Social stratification and mobility in central veracruz

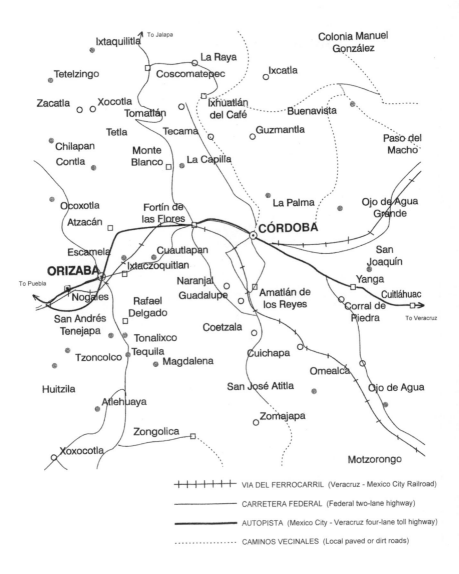

Ixtaquilitla
To Jalapa
Tetelzingo
La Raya
Coscomatepec
Zacatla Xocotla
Tomatlán
Ixhuatlán
del Café
Tetla Tecama
Chilapan
Monte
Blanco La Capilla
Contla
Colonia Manuel
González
Ixcatla
Buenavista
Guzmantla
Paso del
Macho
Ocoxotla
Atzacán
Fortín de
las Flores
La Palma
Ojo de Agua
Grande
Escamela
Cuautlapan
ORIZABA
Ixtaczoquitlan
To Puebla
Nogales
Rafael
Delgado
Naranjal
Guadalupe
Amatlán de
los Reyes
San
Joaquín
Yanga
Cuitláhuac
Corral de
Piedra
To Veracruz
San Andrés
Tenejapa
Coetzala
Tonalixco
Tequila
Tzoncolco Magdalena
Cuichapa
Omealca
Ojo de Agua
Huitzila
Atlehuaya
San José Atitla
Zongolica
Zomajapa
Xoxocotla
Motzorongo

CÓRDOBA

┼┼┼┼┼┼┼ VIA DEL FERROCARRIL (Veracruz - Mexico City Railroad)

───────── CARRETERA FEDERAL (Federal two-lane highway)

━━━━━━━ AUTOPISTA (Mexico City - Veracruz four-lane toll highway)

············· CAMINOS VECINALES (Local paved or dirt roads)

Hugo G. Nutini

Social Stratification and Mobility in Central Veracruz

UNIVERSITY OF TEXAS PRESS
Austin

First edition, 2005

Requests for permission to reproduce material from this
work should be sent to Permissions, University of Texas
Press, Box 7819, Austin, TX 78713-7819.
www.utexas.edu/utpress/about/bpermission.html

♾ The paper used in this book meets the minimum requirements of ANSI/NISO Z39.48-1992 (R1997)
(Permanence of Paper).

Library of Congress Cataloging-in-Publication Data

Nutini, Hugo G.
    Social stratification and mobility in central Veracruz /
Hugo G. Nutini.— 1st ed.
        p.   cm.
    Includes bibliographical references (p.   )
and index.
    ISBN 0-292-70695-2 (cloth : alk. paper)
    1. Social stratification—Mexico—Córdoba Region
(Veracruz-Llave)   2. Social mobility—Mexico—
Córdoba Region (Veracruz-Llave)   3. Córdoba Region
(Veracruz-Llave, Mexico)—Social conditions—
20th century.   I. Title.
HN120.C67N87   2005
305.5'12'072—dc22

                                        2005004643

CONTENTS

$\mathcal{P}$REFACE

$\mathcal{I}$n the summer of 1969 my wife, Jean F. Nutini, and I conducted a survey of the Córdoba-Orizaba region. Our purpose was to map the Nahuatl-speaking population and to determine the general demographic and ethnographic characteristics of the communities and *municipios* (counties) in which Indians were enfranchised. In the course of that summer we also became acquainted with the rural and urban stratification system of the region, and during the next four summers, we collected unsystematic data on the social stratification of the cities of Córdoba and Orizaba. For the next two decades, our work was concentrated in the Tlaxcala-Pueblan Valley and Mexico City, and it was not until twenty years later that we began our systematic study of class formation and mobility in the Córdoba-Orizaba region. For five consecutive summers (1994–1998) we collected the data on which this book is based.

This book stems from our realization that anthropologists working in Mexico have failed to consider social stratification at the regional and national levels. Sociologists have done better; there are a few studies of Mexican social stratification at the national level (Smith 1979; Bartra 1974; Urías et al. 1978; Whetten 1972; Olivé Negrete and Barba de Piña Chán 1960; Alonso 1983), as well as a few specific studies of class (Lomnitz and Pérez Lizaur 1987; Mendizabal 1972; Carrión and Aguilar 1972). This body of literature presents the general parameters of Mexican social stratification either from a quantitative perspective, in the mold of the North American sociological approach to the study of class (adapted to the conditions of a developing country), or from a Marxist perspective. But the literature does not present a clear or coherent picture of class formation, mobility, and the dynamics of stratification—at the national and regional levels—generated by the great changes produced by the Mexican Revolution of 1910. In fact, with the exception of superordinate stratification (the country's haute bourgeoisie, that is, the former landed aristocracy, the new plutocracy, still in the process of formation, and the political class that has run the country since the Revolution and is now undergoing drastic changes), we know little about the class structure of the middle and lower sectors of Mexican society and how they have evolved in the twentieth century.

Given these considerations, a number of questions come to mind. Can the model of North American sociologists be applied to Mexico without significant distortions of empirical reality? Are the principles of stratification in Mexico different from those of modern, industrial nations? What is the effect of expression in class formation and mobility in Mexico — still quite pronounced — as contrasted to those, in the United States, for example, that are significantly less pronounced? How does the ideology of class in Mexico, in contrast to those of more democratically organized societies, affect the configuration of class and mobility? What are the extent of and the reasons for regional variation in the Mexican stratification system? This book contributes to answering these questions.

For the past twenty years we have been primarily engaged in the study of the old landed aristocracy of Mexico, which concentrated in Mexico City and is now on the verge of disappearing as a functioning social class. In our investigation of the survival of the aristocracy after the 1910 Revolution, we have accumulated a significant amount of information on the Mexican stratification system of the country as a whole. This is particularly the case for several provincial cities — near the immense former landed estates — that the aristocracy thoroughly dominated until 1910 and to some extent until the 1934–1940 land reform of President Lázaro Cárdenas, which terminated latifundia in Mexico. By 1960 these local aristocratic ruling nuclei had migrated to Mexico City, where, devoid of their once great wealth, they were able to survive until today. For the past forty-five years, the void left by these ruling elites has been filled by new local plutocracies, which have occasionally contracted social and matrimonial alliances with the few aristocratic families that did not migrate to Mexico City. This is the case with cities such as Puebla, Guadalajara, Querétaro, Jalapa, Oaxaca, Mérida, Córdoba, and Orizaba, since the seventeenth century important centers of aristocratic *hacendados* (latifundia owners). Thus, beginning in the late 1950s, these local elites have emerged as provincial ruling classes that, with a sprinkling of traditional aristocrats, are constituted by new plutocracies whose origins are both foreign (primarily Spanish and Near Eastern — Lebanese, Palestinians, and Syrians — and French and Italian) and domestic (families whose wealth goes back to the late nineteenth century but that are mostly local middle-class and that made their fortunes roughly from 1940 to 1990).

Our research on the Mexican aristocracy produced an ancillary body of data that fairly accurately configures provincial superordinate stratification centered in large and medium-size cities, but the stratification of the middle and lower sectors of society, as far as we were aware, remained largely unknown. This was the state of affairs in the Córdoba-Orizaba region when we began our systematic data collection in 1994. The five summers of fieldwork, then, were dedicated primarily to investigating the middle and lower classes in the orbit of influence of these two medium-size cities.

The substantial Nahuatl-speaking population in several municipios of the region, socially and economically tied to Córdoba and Orizaba, provided the setting for saying something about the Indian transition to Mestizo status, which has been taking place steadily since the end of the armed phase of the Revolution in 1919. One of the main foci of this book is the passage from Indian to Mestizo status in the context of class formation and mobility of regional society. This is not to say that Indian ethnicity has been slighted, only that in the transformation of Indian society, ethnicity must be assessed in the context of class formation focused on the urban environment. To put it differently, ethnicity is not an independent variable in the process of class formation that has been going on for most of the twentieth century. Rather, ethnicity centered exclusively in rural environments has been a sufficient but not a necessary factor in the transformation of regional Indian society.

The ethnographic and quantitative data on which this book is based may be summarized as follows. Most of the participant observation interviewing was done by Hugo G. and Jean F. Nutini. Our field assistants occasionally did open-ended interviewing under our supervision but were particularly helpful in clarifying questions that elicited quantitative data, those pertaining to class affiliation, ethnic identity, interclass relationships, and matters requiring an ideological interpretation of facts. This strategy helped to clarify vague answers or to induce respondents to reflect on unanswered questions. The field assistants were carefully instructed on in-depth interviewing, and their probing often produced surprising information or led to further in-depth interviewing.

The basic ethnographic data on class and mobility, particularly in the urban setting, were generated from ten key informants, who were interviewed for at least fifteen hours each, four of them for more than seventy-five hours. As has been H. Nutini's practice for more than thirteen years of fieldwork since the late 1950s, key informants played a crucial role in providing the cultural consensus model of the ethnographic situation. The final product, of course, emerges when this usually idealized account is actually realized, that is, when additional qualitative and quantitative information is assessed. With respect to the present book, it is toward this goal that the quantitative data obtained from questionnaires were essential.

We made extensive use of group interviewing, usually three to five informants of the same sex, having learned long ago that group interviews yield the best results when men and women are interviewed separately. As children are important sources of information on differences between group ideology and how the social system works in practice, we also interviewed them whenever possible.

Most of the quantitative data were gathered by the administration of two questionnaires. One contained twenty-five questions on name, sex, age, residence, education, and profession or occupation and general information on class and mobility (ranging from class membership and awareness to interclass relationships to knowledge of other classes, changes that have taken place during the past fifty years, and the social and economic conditions that have been instrumental in social and/or ethnic mobility). Another questionnaire explored in greater depth questions on the class membership of respondents' parents, factors that made it possible to achieve their present class position, awareness of other people's class membership, characteristic class behavior and lifestyles, the significance of education, residence, occupation or profession, and other factors involved in class formation and mobility. The two questionnaires were phrased differently for administering to the urban superordinate sector (the rich and powerful and the upper middle class) and all urban and rural classes. (The rationale for this research strategy of generating quantitative data is implicit in the text, especially in chapters 3 and 4.)

Other quantitative data were gathered by the administration of eight- to ten-item questionnaires to opportunity samples of urban respondents on specific topics. Finally, male and female respondents were asked to complete self-awareness tests, card-sorting tasks, clustering tasks, and identification and correlation tasks.

*T*he fieldwork research was made possible by a series of small grants. From the University of Pittsburgh we received four grants from the Center for Latin American Studies and one grant each from the University Center for International Studies, Faculty of Arts and Sciences, Center for Social and Urban Research, and

Central Research Development Fund. In addition, we received grants-in-aid from the American Philosophical Society, the Wenner-Gren Foundation for Anthropological Research, and the Jacobs Fund of Bellingham, Washington. We are very grateful to these institutions for their generous financial help, without which our work in the Córdoba-Orizaba region would not have been possible.

It is difficult to single out every individual and institution that, in one way or another, helped us to write this book and carry out the fieldwork on which it is based, but we would like to express our appreciation to those that made the most significant contributions. To the municipal authorities of the cities of Fortin de las Flores, Córdoba, Orizaba, Coscomatepec, and San Juan de la Punta, we are grateful for administrative support. We are intellectually and professionally indebted to John M. Roberts, Barry L. Isaac, Doren L. Slade, Lisa Moscowitz, Leonard Plotnicov, L. Keith Brown, Richard Scaglion, Marc Bermann, David Robichaux, and Timothy D. Murphy, who read parts of the text, made constructive criticisms, suggested changes in style, presentation, and organization, or discussed theoretical or methodological matters.

We are grateful to the countless municipal authorities of the Córdoba-Orizaba communities where information was collected for their openness and willingness to help and for the time and effort they devoted to establishing the proper conditions for fieldwork. Our chief informants in the cities of Fortin de las Flores and Córdoba are Orquidea Alvarez, Juan Landt, the late Daniel Rabago, Rubén Calatayud, Luisa Albuerne, Cecilia Frizzi, Silvester Hernandez, Alicia Ramirez, Federico Massieu, and Gloria Fagoaga de Massieu.

We also want to express our gratitude for the generosity and availability of our informants in the many rural communities in which we collected information. To the more than twenty ritual kinsmen (*compadres, comadres, ahijados,* and *ahijadas*) whom we have contacted in the region during the past twenty-five years, we can only say that the deep bonds between us have been an important source for the subtler aspects of class, ethnicity, and mobility.

And we are very grateful to the three main interviewers, Carlos Altamira, Federico Massieu, and Laura Carpio, who administered the two extensive questionnaires that generated most of the quantitative data on which this book is based. They did a splendid, accurate job in the onerous work that this task entails.

SOCIAL STRATIFICATION AND MOBILITY IN CENTRAL VERACRUZ

| **THE MEXICAN STRATIFICATION SYSTEM**

Class Formation, Mobility, and the Changing Perspective

*T*he social stratification of Mexico has changed greatly since the Mexican Revolution of 1910. It has evolved toward the type of class system associated with developed countries; and today, at least formally, it is not so different from that of the United States. The Mexican Revolution did not bring democracy to the country, as was the earnest expectation of the population, but it did bring about a reorganization of society from top to bottom. (Notably, this was done almost entirely within the framework of civilian rule. After the armed phase of the Revolution, which ended in 1919, the new political class neutralized the armed forces, something that no subsequent revolutionary movement in Latin America was able to do in the twentieth century.) The rural sectors of the country were transformed from being part of an oppressive seigneurialism into a fluid population of free peasants, with hopes of a better existence, hopes that, unfortunately, not even the 1934–1940 land reform was able to fulfill. However, the policy of Indianism fostered by the government, and actively implemented by dedicated personnel in the educational system and by several agencies in various branches of government functioning as cultural brokers, gave rural people pride in their Indian past and new ways to organize their lives.[1]

The urban middle classes, though few in number, increasingly enjoyed better educational and economic opportunities. Freed from the influences and control of the superordinate tradition (undue subservience to and respect for the holders of social, economic, and political power), particularly in provincial cities, they experienced significant mobility and by midcentury had basically acquired the characteristics of the middle classes in industrial societies. The superordinate class, essentially enfranchised in Mexico City, was radically restructured: the aristocracy lost all power and wealth and at the provincial level disappeared as a functioning social class. Revolutionaries with no ties to the old Porfirian regime became the political class of the country. After one term in high office—the result of the paramount slogan of the Revolution, "Sufragio efectivo y no reelección"—Effective suffrage and no reelection (the first part of which was never complied with, whereas the second part was strictly enforced)—they were transformed into entrepreneurial magnates. An assortment of bankers, industrialists, and businessmen became the ruling class of the country, and in the past two decades many became billionaires.

At the state level, essentially the same situation obtained, and countless provincial cities and their surrounding regions became a reflection of the stratification system of Mexico City. Indeed, this bare outline of the evolution of Mexican society may be regarded as a gestalt of the transformation brought about by the first popular revolution of the twentieth century that transformed a seigneurial, backward society and guided its first steps toward a modern industrial country. Flawed in many ways, and unable to fulfill the aspirations of most Mexicans for a more just society, the Revolution nonetheless was a great leap forward. Its significance is most clearly realized when one considers that it took place so early in the century, when there were no models available. The goals and aspirations of revolutionary leaders became those of similar movements that arose more than a generation later in Latin American countries with large Indian populations. The essential significance of the Mexican Revolution was not what it accomplished at home but that it served as a symbol, and to some extent a model, that shaped revolutionary movements in the Western Hemisphere throughout the century.

Scaling down the problem, in these introductory remarks I wish to put in historical perspective how the Mexican Revolution was instrumental in transforming the stratification system of the city of Córdoba and its surrounding region in the second half of the century. First, it is of paramount importance to understand the realignment of classes that took place after the institutional structure of the *ancien régime* ceased to have dominance and a more egalitarian context came into being. Thus the following remarks focus on the consequences of the restructuring that the local superordinate sector has undergone and on the changes in social mobility and economic fluidity that affected the middle and lower sectors of society.

THE CONJOINED EFFECT OF THE POLITICAL AND RULING CLASSES

Probably for ideological reasons, twentieth-century social scientists have paid little attention to what I have termed superordinate stratification.

In the case of Mexico, to be sure, sociologists and historians, and occasionally anthropologists, have written about the plutocracy (usually referred to as oligarchy, which, in a Marxist view, has a distinctly deprecatory connotation), the political class, and the "burguesía" (bourgeoisie, denoting essentially the haute bourgeoisie), a hopelessly imprecise term. About the aristocracy, the moribund sector of the superordinate class, little has been written by social scientists that is sociologically sound and divested of ideological bias. The sole exception, as far as I am aware, is Takie Sugiyama Lebra's (1993) ethnography of the contemporary Japanese aristocracy. When social scientists must necessarily refer to or inevitably discuss superordinate groups, they do it reluctantly and with a tinge of antipathy, a latent manifestation of antagonism toward any group that is or has been in a position of exploitation of another segment of society. Considerable numbers of historians are the exception; rising above personal beliefs and ideological considerations, they have given unbiased accounts of superordinate groups (e.g., Schama 1989).

In my historical and ethnographic studies of the Mexican aristocracy (Nutini 1995, 2004), one of the basic analytical premises was that to understand and explain a social stratification system, it is necessary to have detailed knowledge of the superordinate class. The rationale is simple. As the holders of most power and wealth and occupying the most exalted social positions, the perceptions they engender among the middle and lower classes and the influence they exercise affect the structure of society from top to bottom. From this perspective, one could no more understand the stratification of nineteenth-century Mexico without reference to the aristocracy and the *hacienda* system than one could comprehend the contemporary class system of Mexico without reference to the plutocracy and the ruling political party of the country. The justification for this stance has a necessary structural and a sufficient expressive component that complement each other.

Elsewhere (Nutini 1995), I defined the concept of superordinate class as being composed of three main sectors: the aristocracy, the plutocracy, and the political class. For the structural analysis of the Mexican stratification system today, the aristocracy is only tangentially significant historically. Until the Revolution, the aristocracy played an important role in provincial stratification, as it controlled many of the largest cities and surrounding regions where its haciendas were located. Its influence lingered on until the 1934–1940 land reform, but from then on most aristocratic hacendados, who were the main factor in the organization of the social and, to a significant extent, the economic life of many regions of the country, quickly vanished from the local scene. By the early 1950s provincial aristocrats had almost entirely concentrated in Mexico City, and their influence in regional affairs was essentially to have created a vacuum that was filled by new social and economic superordinate groups. Thus the new plutocracy and political class of revolutionary origin was composed of the two superordinate sectors that were most instrumental in creating the class system with which this study is concerned.

Throughout most of the century, the political class that began to emerge immediately after the Revolution and came to fruition in the late 1920s never lost sight of transforming Mexico into a more fluid and equitable society. Many politicians throughout the country worked to improve the lot of the dispossessed; they were dedicated social revolutionaries. Despite the personal and collective corruption that came to characterize the political class, from the highest levels of the federal system (the executive and legislative branches) to manifold positions in local state government, most of its members worked toward promoting opportunities for the disadvantaged and creating an atmosphere of positive expectation. For nearly forty years (from the early 1930s to the late 1960s), the country made great improvements in education, social security, health, transportation, and communication, creating the basic infrastructure for a modern industrial complex. However, the ruling party, the Partido Revolucionario Institucional (PRI, the embodiment of the political class, around which a vast system of patronage evolved), was never able to foster political democracy; thus from the local community to the highest levels of the federal government, the country was a benevolent civil dictatorship. The PRI brooked no political dissent, and either by bribing or co-opting dissenters into the party, it reigned supreme. Only at the lowest village level was there a measure of democracy, but as one ascended to levels of increasing demographic complexity (to town, city, state, and nation), the system became more oppressive.

The system worked reasonably well until the late 1960s, and undoubtedly the majority of the population supported the ruling party, regardless of the corruption about which most fairly well educated citizens were aware. Indeed, up to that point, the postrevolutionary political class had done a very creditable job of transforming the country from semifeudal conditions into reasonably modern ones, and the oppressive and occasionally tyrannical methods it employed could perhaps be justified. Largely as a result of policies that promoted education and economic development that the PRI genuinely promoted, the system began to falter as the population at large became more politically conscious and no longer willing to overlook the rampant corruption. Had the PRI begun to liberalize and promote political pluralism, as it appeared to be doing during the presidency of Adolfo López Mateos (1958–1964), it would have been a tremendous achievement, and the majority of the population would have forgiven and forgotten the oppression and corruption it had taken to bring the country to the verge of being a modern industrial nation. Unfortunately, it is rarely the case that individuals or groups give up power voluntarily. Mexico had to endure another thirty-five years of political chicanery, and the ruling party fought democratic reform by all available means whenever it was challenged. On the whole, for many years, the PRI served the country well, and the very success of the policies it espoused was the source of its decline as the undisputed ruling party, leading ultimately to a democratization of the political system that has not yet been entirely achieved.

But how was the political class of the country instrumental in causing the realignment of classes that has significantly modified the stratification system? Before answering this question, let me specify who are the members of the political class at the national, state, and local (urban) levels.

Directly until the late 1930s and indirectly since then, the new political class has enjoyed undisputed political power since 1929, when the PRI came into existence. At any one time, it includes living past presidents, cabinet members, some prominent members of congress (senators, *diputados,* or congressmen), most state governors, and assorted high office holders. The political class during President Miguel Alemán Valdez's tenure (1946–1952) had about 1,500 members, and it has grown at the rate of roughly 150 every six-year administration, leading to close to 3,000 by the administration of President Ernesto Zedillo Ponce de León (1994–2000). Given the principle of no-reelection instituted by the Revolution, a politician's career culminated in a high office to which he could not be reelected. After holding high office, members of this circle have continued to have influence, and for nearly three generations, a fairly permanent nucleus has guaranteed the continuity and stability of the political class. Perhaps more significant is that the Revolution did not change the tradition, dating back to colonial times, of high political office as an important source of enrichment. In the twentieth century some of the largest fortunes in Mexico have had their origins in politics. The result of this form of nearly institutionalized corruption is that sooner or later politicians become plutocrats and members of the ruling class.

Corruption enriches not only the individual office holder but also the many families related to him or her by ties of kinship, *compadrazgo,* and friendship. Indeed, in every administration since President Alemán's, at least five thousand families have been the recipients of the profits of political corruption and have joined the lower and middle ranks of the plutocracy. Thus, at the national or local level, these members become part of the ruling class. As ruling party control is coming to an end and the political system is becoming more representative and democratic, politics as a source of wealth is being curtailed; but the role of the political class in the formation of the ruling class cannot be underestimated. It must be noted, however, that the effect of politicians as they are transformed into members of the ruling class is realized differently. Officials at the federal level and governors of the richest states have the greatest effect as members of the ruling class, as almost invariably they join the richest plutocratic groups. By contrast, at the state and local levels (cities and municipios), politicians are more effective as members of the political class than as plutocrats of lower stature. (Implicit in this categorization is the popular belief, well documented by evidence, that the higher the political office, the more there is to plunder and the richer politicians become.) By "effect," as I discuss more fully below, I mean the direct or indirect influence of the political-ruling class on the population at large in fostering mobility and a more egalitarian society, which ironically is the result of corruption. Be this as it may, the local political-ruling class is a mirror image of the national model, and only the scale of power and corruption is different (see Chapter 3).

Given the ultimate fission of the political and ruling classes, particularly during the past thirty years due primarily to the increasing democratization of society, it is best to analyze these superordinate classes as a single sector and point out differences and similarities when necessary. During the period of gestation of Mexico's twentieth-century plutocracy, roughly from 1920 to 1940, the early great fortunes were made by politicians, and just a few years later, in fact, President Alemán became the first plutocratic magnate to emerge after the Revolution. Soon after, diversification took place and plutocrats of nonpolitical extraction amassed the largest fortunes and became increasingly powerful. At this point, no later than the late 1950s, one may speak of a ruling class of plutocratic magnates essentially independent from the political class. This is the basic realignment of classes that took place essentially at the superordinate level, which since then has been extended to the middle and lower sectors of society. Building on the foundations provided by the Revolution for nearly two generations (promoting education, pride in acknowledging the Indian component of being Mexican, and in general fostering an open society), the restructuring of the superordinate sector has become instrumental in realigning all classes of society, most notably at the state and local levels.

In the capital and the largest urban centers, where are concentrated the best-educated and politically conscious segments of the country's population, the model of upward mobility and economic aspiration was the plutocratic magnate who, by dint of ability, hard work, and foresight, has inspired the middle sectors of society to become entrepreneurs, dedicated followers of capitalism, and desirous of improving their social position. The fluidity of modern Mexico after midcentury provided, of course, the structural conditions for the actualization of this model, but the immediate sources of its realization were successful, visible plutocrats. The tremendous proliferation of fairly wealthy merchants, manufacturers, small- to medium-scale industrialists, and all sorts of middle-class entrepreneurs during the past generation are the vicarious emulators of plutocratic magnates, rightly perceived as emerging from similar class positions to great wealth and high social standing. To put it differently, social and economic mobility, from the lower to the middle rungs of society and on to the superordinate sector, has been the result of the confluence of modernization fostered by the Revolution and a capitalist model that it never contemplated obliterating. Small as the middle class of the country is compared with that of industrial nations, it is an important factor in the restructuring of stratification in the second half of the century, which in feedback fashion became instrumental in the overall fluidity of Mexican society. By contrast, politicians do not elicit the same vicarious emulation; they are unremittingly resented, given that the middle classes are the most politically conscious sector of the population. Nevertheless, the entrepreneurial success of the middle class served as a model for the bulk of the urban working classes (excluding the professional sector, which is perceived as another avenue of upward social and economic mobility).

Over the past twenty years, the political class, traditionally the PRI, has come to include the opposition parties (most prominently, the Partido de Acción Nacional, PAN, and the Partido de la Revolución Democratica, PRD). These opposition parties have similarly affected a different segment of the population, mostly the less educated working-class sectors, at the state and local levels, particularly in small and medium-size cities.

This different mode of vicarious emulation has two sources. First, most members of the political class (important, visible politicians) are of humbler origin than plutocratic magnates, and the working class is more likely to identify with the former than with the latter. Being less aware of the aura of corruption that politicians elicit among the more educated, or simply caring less, they identify with politicians, not infrequently bordering on hero worship. This syndrome can be traced back to colonial times. It may be defined as a kind of sociopsychological *caciquismo,* that is, a strong attachment to a leader as a patron and as a source of economic well-being. This is a deeply ingrained Mexican trait that affects many public domains of behavior. For example, it explains the identification of hacienda peons with former landowners, despite the exploitation that bound them. Caciquismo, so defined, is still strongly present among the working classes and lower orders of society. In my opinion, it has created a psychological dependency that fosters an inability to think and behave independently, resulting in grave consequences for the development of the concept of citizen, which is a necessary condition for the organization of a modern nation. Time and again in my research in urban environments in central Mexico, I have encountered this dependency on specific members of the political class, which brings us to the second source of emulation, exemplified by the American notion of the local boy who made good, that justifies and reinforces the first, as follows.

Most politicians are well known locally and serve as a source of patronage before ultimately becoming members of the political class; even if they remain only locally prominent, they fulfill the same function. Indeed, it is in this kind of subsidiary role that politicians are most effective as models of mobility and as influencing the dispossessed to strive for social and economic improvement. Subliminally, this is the perception that local politicians project, with little perception of the corruption and opportunism that the more educated public (always the minority) attributes to them. Innumerable times I have heard the following expression about a politician who leaves office with a reputation for fiscal honesty: "¡Que pendejo, estuvo en el poder y no robó nada!" (What a fool, he did not steal while in office!). This, of course, says a great deal about the subject and object of this popular expression—the insidiousness of institutionalized corruption and the willingness of the dispossessed to identify themselves with leaders regardless of ethical considerations.

It is one of the paradoxes of the Mexican Revolution that the political and ruling classes it ultimately forged entailed a strange mixture of capitalist and socialist ideas. On the one hand, there is a continuation of the old nineteenth-century entente that characterized the relationship between the ruling and political class (the unspoken agreement to rule in the economic and the political domain respectively without interference); on the other hand, basic social, economic, and material reforms have been implemented that were not necessarily advantageous to the economic interests of the rich and powerful in a developing capitalist system. This has essentially been the dilemma that has characterized the role of the ruling and political classes in Mexico in the postrevolutionary period. Although irrational and inherently flawed, the single or joint effect of ruling-political action has been determinant in transforming Mexico for nearly ninety years.

FLUIDITY OF THE STRATIFICATION SYSTEM DURING THE PAST GENERATION AND THE REALIGNMENT OF CLASSES

The transformation that the Mexican middle classes have been undergoing for most of the century has been paralleled in the lower sectors of society. This has been most significant in the passage from Indian to Mestizo status. At the onset of the Revolution of 1910, the Indian population was about 40 percent of the total population of Mexico; by 1950 it had been reduced to about 20 percent; today, it stands at less than 10 percent. This dramatic transformation, unparalleled among Latin American countries with similar demographic composition (Peru, Bolivia, Ecuador, Paraguay), bears witness to the Revolution's success in modernizing the country and creating the ambience, if not necessarily the most propitious conditions, for upward socioeconomic mobility, which in this context inevitably means the ultimate disappearance of the Indian as a distinct ethnic category (Nutini 1997). My focus here, however, is on the great rural and urban masses that are the direct result of this ethnic transformation of the country.

A ninety-two-year-old, well-educated lawyer and former city official described the contrast between the 1910s and 1990s as follows:

Me acuerdo muy bien lo cerrada que era la sociedad cordobesa durante la revolución. Un pequeño grupo de familias de seis o siete hacendados, con un séquito de una veintena de familias que dominaban el comercio de la ciudad, controlaban la vida social y ecónomica de la región. Unos cuantos profesionales, médicos y abogados, que les rendian pleitesía, constituian lo que hoy día se llama la clase media. Casi toda la población la constituian los obreros urbanos y las grandes masas rurales de peones, en su mayor parte indígenas de las haciendas, pequeñas propiedades, y comunidades independientes de la región.

En tales condiciones de total dominación, las diferencias existentes entre las masas campesinas y urbanas no se podian considerar como diferentes clases sociales. !Que diferencia de como estan las cosas hoy día! En primer lugar, las comunidades indígenas que hasta la revolución casi llegaban hasta la periferia de la ciudad, entonces con cerca de 35,000 habitantes, ya no existen; han dejado de hablar Náhuatl; y fuera de algunas costumbres que todavía persistent, se han totalmente transformado. En Córdoba, ahora con más de 350,000 habitantes, como igualmente Orizaba, las oportunidades de todo tipo han atraido a muchísima gente de toda la región. El crecimiento de la ciudad se ha debido principalmente a los muchos negocios que se han venido estableciendo desde principios de los años 50 por hombre de negocios locales, españoles, libaneses, palestinos, y mexicanos de Puebla y México. Creo yo que esta es la razón principal de la fluidez económica y social que ha experimentado la ciudad. Sin las trabas y prejuicios tradicionals que caracterizaban a la sociedad mexicana, que en su mayor parte eliminó la revolución, la sociedad cordobesa ha evolucionado hasta el punto en que cualquier individuo, sin importar su origen social o étnico, puede aspirar a una mejor vida si está dispuesto a trabajar y comportarse debidamente.

(I remember very well how close Córdoba's society was during [the armed phase of] the Revolution. A small group of six or seven hacendado families, with a retinue of 20 or so families which dominated the city's commerce, controlled the social and economic life of the region. A few professionals, physicians and lawyers, socially subservient to them, constituted what today is called the middle class. Almost the entire population was composed of urban workers and the great rural masses of peons, mostly Indians, in the haciendas, smallholdings, and independent communities of the region. Under such conditions of total domination, the differences between the peasants and urban masses could not be considered different social classes. What a difference considering how things are today! In the first place, the Indian communities that until the Revolution were located almost at the periphery of the city, then with about 35,000 inhabitants, no longer exist; they do not speak Nahuatl anymore and except for some customs that still survive, have been totally transformed. In Córdoba, now with more than 350,000 inhabitants, as well as Orizaba [10 miles away], opportunities of all kinds have attracted a great many people from all over the region. The growth of the city has been due mainly to the many enterprises that have steadily been established since the early fifties by local businessmen, Spaniards, Lebanese, Palestinians, and Mexicans from Puebla and Mexico City. I believe this is the main reason for the economic and social fluidity that the city has experienced. Without the traditional impediments and prejudices that characterized Mexican society, which were mostly eliminated by the Revolution, Córdoba's society has evolved to the point that any individual, regardless of social and ethnic origin, may aspire to a better life if he is willing to work and behave properly.)

I have elicited similar assessments from other elderly informants in cities in the states of Tlaxcala, Puebla, Hidalgo, and Mexico; with some variations, it applies to most city-regions of the country. In addition, this informant's perceptive statement was confirmed by hundreds of interviews conducted in Córdoba, Orizaba, and Fortin. It highlights three basic points. First, a large segment of the population has moved from Indian to Mestizo status. Those who subsequently migrate to the city, in turn, become an influence in rural environments and ultimately are reconstituted as the matrix for the global realignment of classes. Second, the rigidity of traditional Mexican society—dominance of a small group of aristocrats, a budding plutocracy of merchants, a minuscule middle class of professionals, and the overwhelming majority of the population that constitutes an undifferentiated class—determined the stratification of the city. Third, the tendency toward a more open society fostered by the Revolution resulted in the second part of the century in a class system approaching that of modern nations.

Fundamentally, Mexican social stratification has evolved into a fluid, mobile system that to a significant degree parallels that of the United States, as it has been described and analyzed by sociologists. This generalization needs to be qualified, however. It is not only that the Revolution unfettered a society mired in the traditions of an estatelike system, but, as inadequately as the political class has performed, it promoted economic development and the general industrialization of the country. Thus it is the case that sufficient liberalization of the social system was conditioned by necessary economic development and that this became the context in which a fluid, mobile class has developed. Since the leadership of the Revolution and its successors never envisioned a socialist, classless state but implicitly condoned the creation of a capitalist society, the class system that Mexico developed (along with most Latin American countries and many others throughout the world as they emerged from colonialism) is an inevitable result. By asserting that the stratification system of Mexico parallels that of the United States, I mean that the forms but not necessarily the content and actualization of social classes are similar. While one may speak of middle and lower classes in Mexico, their configurations are not the same as those of the United States in terms of comparative affluence, opportunity for mobility, and consciousness of kind. Essentially the differences rest on economic affluence, industrialization, and degree of political democracy. Assuming that the United States and all democratic industrialized countries in the world have essentially the same class system, it may be asked, at what point of democratization and industrialization has a developing country, like Mexico, achieved the same class system? Below I address elements of this question.

By any standard, and probably since the middle of the century, Mexico has had the infrastructure of a modern nation: a well-organized banking system, an effective industrial complex, a good system of communication and transportation, an up-to-date educational establishment, a social security system (that on paper is as good and humane as the best of any industrial nation), and, on the whole, all the institutional structure of an advanced nation-state. In addition, Mexico is a country rich in natural resources. Why, then, has Mexico not achieved the status of a modern industrial nation, with a corresponding class system? The easy answer is to blame it all on lack of political democracy and the corruption of the political class. In my estimation, there are three other factors that are seldom mentioned by historians and political scientists. The first is the deeply ingrained trait in Mexican society that beyond the categories of kinsman, ritual kinsman, neighbor, and friend, no other significant tie is recognized as effectively binding people together. This is part of the colonial inheritance that continued after Independence under the seigneurialism that characterized Mexican society in the nineteenth century, which has been instrumental in retarding the development of citizenship as the primary building block of a modern nation. The second is that citizenship takes many generations to create; with the sole exception of Japan, it took at least five generations to develop in the modern industrial nations of the world. It is thus not surprising that in Mexico (and in most countries with a colonial past), where several aspects of the estate system survived until the twentieth century, the concept of citizenship has taken so long to develop. The third factor is the broad pattern of corruption that goes beyond the political domain and permeates much of Mexican society. Corruption permeates most domains of public interaction, it is taken as a necessary given to get things done, and nobody tries to stop corruption where this might be possible.

Implicit here is the concept of civic society, which Antonio Gramsci coined to refer to public and implicitly organized social life that is noneconomic and nongovernmental, for which he has not received proper credit, as Robson (2000, 14) points out. It is in this denotation that the concept of civic society frames the weak sense of citizenship exhibited by most Mexicans of all social classes and by many social scientists since the early 1930s (Martin 1998, 65–73). The chapters that follow illustrate Gramsci's notion that there are two distinguishing features of the state and social forces within it, namely, civil needs and governmental ideological domination. This often creates tension and does not result in societal benefits.

In manifold forms and contexts, these factors affect the realization of a de jure equitable socioeconomic, political system. It allows for the undue concentration of power and wealth to a degree intolerable in a democratic industrial state; it creates an atmosphere of impotence and resignation that impedes effective political action and curtails economic access to resources. Those who have been fortunate to make it into the middle classes have become complacent and passively accept the state of affairs of everyone else. Most damaging, this state of affairs leads to numerous forms of exploitation of the working classes, from factory workers and farmworkers to domestic help and store clerks. The great majority of the population, those struggling to rise on the economic scale and the dispossessed, wait for leadership that would redeem them. This may appear to be a reification, but it characterizes much of the politicoeconomic ambience of the country. However, as the people are becoming politically more aware and economically knowledgeable about managing the system, this traditional state of affairs is receding rather rapidly, and people at all levels of society are actively participating in the more open society of Mexico that has been evolving during the past decade.[2]

What does the new realignment of classes mean? Essentially, during the past forty years, there has been significant upward socioeconomic mobility from the lower ranks of society to the lower end of the middle sector. The dispossessed are increasingly entering the specialized working class (as factory workers and various kinds of technical shop owners) and the service industry (as small shop owners, barbers, and tailors and in the innumerable occupations that are intrinsic to the urbanization that has occurred over the past fifty years). What has not happened is that the professional classes (from physicians, lawyers, and engineers to all other occupations requiring a university education) are not proportionally increasing the ranks of the affluent middle class, and, structurally and expressively, many of them remain members of the working class. University students are the most educated and socially and politically aware sector of the population, but they also become the most frustrated when, on graduation, their aspirations for a better life are thwarted by not finding the appropriate job in industry or commerce. So far this has been the most serious failure of the public and private sectors of the economy, particularly when, at the end of President Luis Echeverría Alvarez's administration (1970–1976), the government forecasted unprecedented prosperity. This has not come to pass, and the middle class, as the most affected by the downturn of the economy, has remained stagnant. Thus social mobility has been uneven.

What, then, has propelled upward mobility in the lower sectors of society? This is a difficult question to answer, but in my opinion two factors have certainly had a significant effect: secondary education and permanent migration to the city. The expansion of secondary education, both in urban and in rural environments, has been determined by providing the underclasses with a modicum of knowledge concerning the form and context of the industrial-mercantile world as the main source of making a living, not to mention the rudiments of science and technology that this process entails. Without this educational background, the transition from rural to urban life would have been more difficult, and not nearly as many people would have achieved economically rewarding working-class status. Thus education provided the necessary conditions for upward mobility, whereas urban migration constitutes the sufficient conditions for the realization of this phenomenon. The spectacular growth of urbanization—as much as a four- or fivefold increase in the population of many cities in less than forty years, has facilitated the growth of the economy; more significantly, it has become a model of expectations for the poorest rural populations. In the city the majority prospered, but many remained dispossessed, particularly in Mexico City, living in deplorable slum conditions not infrequently worse than those they left behind.

Perhaps more significant has been the effect of urbanization on rural communities, from traditional Indian to secularized Mestizo villages. The main factor in this transformation has been community-centered labor migration. In the Tlaxcala-Pueblan Valley, for example, hundreds of villages since the early 1950s have become extensions of the city and their populations transformed from peasantry to a proletariat working class. The same may probably be documented for many regions, which, together with permanent migration to the city (particularly Mexico City, Guadalajara, Monterrey, Ciudad Juárez, Tijuana, and Puebla), accounts for the great working-class transformation of Mexico. Only a few of the most isolated areas, so-called regions of refuge (Chiapas, the Sierra de Puebla, the Huasteca Potosina, and a few others), have remained relatively unaffected.

What I have outlined is essentially the emergence of a lower-middle class as described by sociologists in the United States, including the distinction between white- and blue-collar workers. This is a diagnostic point that warrants more discussion.

Let me begin by saying that the overall realignment of classes of Mexican society since the Revolution of 1910 must be focused, as it has by social scientists in the United States, on both the so-called objective and subjective approaches to stratification. The first is exemplified by the Lynd and Lynd study, *Middletown, USA* (1937), in which the criteria of classification are power, wealth, education, residence, occupation, and so on, and the emphasis is on the differential attribution of these criteria in a changing society. The second, as exemplified by Warner's *Yankee City* (1942, 1963) series, stresses the behavioral and expressive attributes of class, where lineage, heredity, local prominence, and appropriate breeding play significant roles. These contrasting approaches are not exclusive; on the contrary, they must be differentially employed. The closed, seigneurial-like stratification system of Mexico before the Revolution is best exemplified by the subjective approach, as expressive behavior, lineage, and heredity were of paramount importance in classifying people in the upper and middle sectors of society and in keeping the great masses of the population under control. This does not mean that some objective criteria were not at work, such as political domination, economic exploitation, and lack of access to education for the majority. By contrast, the open, more fluid stratification system that emerged after the Revolution must be explained in terms of the objective approach, given that the subjective criteria's constraints have been greatly diminished even as some subjective criteria remain in place. A few examples can clarify the matter.

First, white-collar workers rank higher than blue-collar workers in the class scale, posited on the notion that nonmanual work is more prestigious and reputable than manual work. Thus office workers and nurses are ranked higher than mechanics and factory workers, even though the latter make significantly more money than the former. This is a pervasive syndrome that structures many domains of social interaction in the lower sectors of society and shapes the configuration of mobility. Second, caciquismo and the relationship of dependence it creates are still very much a part of the sociopolitical process in the lower sectors of society. This form of the patron-client relationship implicitly asserts that there are individuals who are inherently to be regarded as superordinately placed, to whom the subordinately placed must attach themselves in order to get on in the world. It also lends itself to exploitation, which the dispossessed implicitly accept in order to gain some, mostly minimal, benefice. Third, there is an old saying that illustrates an important principle of Mexican social interaction: "Juntos pero no revueltos." Essentially, the saying states that people may gather together but must maintain social barriers and distinctions. This syndrome (a survival of the estate-like organization of society before the Revolution) continues to structure much of the interaction of people at all levels of society and perpetuates traditional patterns of interaction in terms of positions of superiority and inferiority, leading to the fostering of unwarranted respect for persons in superordinate social positions.[3] All three are diagnostic examples of the survival of the subjective criteria that characterize Mexico's new class structure in the second half of the century. I shall have much more to say about these matters in the next chapter.

In conclusion, we may characterize the stratification system of Mexico in the second half of the century as evolving toward a class realignment similar to that of modern industrial nations. The transformation has been uneven: great at the bottom, slow in the middle, and perceptibly different but static at the top. Structurally, the main impediment for more mobility into the middle classes has been the lack of economic opportunities, while the dispossessed continue to move into the working classes as the result of the increasing industrialization of the country, which provides jobs better remunerated than mere subsistence. The superordinate class, it goes without saying, is the most similar to that of industrialized countries. With the exception of the superordinate sector, class consciousness has been slow in developing, and the lower the social scale, the less developed it is. This is understandable, as the same phenomenon obtained in the transition from estate to class in Europe after the demise of the ancien régime until the second half of the nineteenth century, by which time a class system was solidly in place. Quite often in the working sector of the population there is ambivalence about class membership, particularly among those who have been recently co-opted and those who are on the verge of making the transition to the middle classes. There are evidently regional variations, but as far as I have been able to determine, this ambivalence increases as one moves from the great urban centers to provincial city environments.

This is the general environment that characterizes the social stratification system of the city of Córdoba, which is typical of many medium-size cities in central Mexico.

	$\mathcal{A}$ COMBINED STRUCTURAL AND
Chapter 1	EXPRESSIVE APPROACH TO THE STUDY
	OF SOCIAL STRATIFICATION

*T*he basic assumption of this book is that structural variables alone give an incomplete account of social stratification and mobility. Rather, these phenomena are understood and explained when there is a complementation of structural and expressive variables. In two books on the Mexican aristocracy and plutocracy (Nutini 1995, 2004), I demonstrate the complementarity of the objective and subjective foci as the most efficient analytical tool for approaching the study of class formation, social mobility, and persistence in the superordinate sectors of society. In this chapter I briefly put in perspective what the structural-expressive focus entails as it applies to the middle and lower sectors of society and the differences involved compared to the study of superordinate stratification.

THE STUDY OF STRATIFICATION IN HISTORICAL PERSPECTIVE

Since sociology became an academic discipline more than a century ago, society's groups, particularly stratification, have received as much attention as kinship has received in anthropology. The golden age of sociological studies of class, mobility, and other aspects of stratification occurred between 1920 and 1960, when, stimulated by what are now considered classical theories and positions, sociologists postulated new approaches, debated old issues, and occasionally formulated new theories. Since the reprint of Bendix and Lipset's (1966) volume on class, status, and power, stratification studies have received little attention, and no theoretical innovations, let alone theories, have been postulated. This decline in stratification studies may be related to the overall decline of the Marxist and functional paradigms and the inordinate concern of sociology over the past twenty-five years with practical problems and quantifying methodologies. It should be noted that with a few exceptions, most notably W. Lloyd Warner, anthropologists have not contributed significantly to the study of stratification.

Be this as it may, by 1940 expression had become an important component of studies of social class and mobility. This trend was initiated by Warner in his emphasis on the behavioral aspects of class and represented a reaction against Marxism's exclusively structural definition of class. Thus by midcentury stratification studies had become polarized between the "objective" and the "subjective" approach. Granted that these labels are biased and misleading, they do entail different criteria in defining the various forms of stratification. The objective, or structural, approach emphasizes criteria such as power, wealth, education, occupation, and residence. It is exemplified by the work of Robert Lynd and Helen Lynd (1937) on a midwestern city, in which the main emphasis of class is on the dynamics of social mobility and the differential attribution of power and wealth in a changing society. The subjective approach stresses the behavioral and expressive aspects of class. Warner is its most notable proponent; he rejects the conceptualization of class on purely objective criteria and emphasizes the expressive, ritual, and more permanent (lineage and heredity) aspects of class. This is clear in his definition of a class system as "two or more orders of people who are believed to be, and are accordingly ranked by members of the community, in socially superior and inferior positions" (Warner 1963, 32).

It should be noted, however, that the objective definition of class and mobility is the most widely accepted, both among social scientists and among the general public. With the possible exception of Great Britain, where the people in general are still very much aware of lineage and tradition, in modern industrial countries the subjective components of stratification are not easily visualized and remain largely sub rosa. I attribute this awareness, or lack of it, to the lingering effect of the estate system: the more national societies have transcended it, the more likely they are to perceive class in purely objective terms. In Mexico, for example, subjective criteria still play a significant role in classifying people, not unlike in Great Britain. The situation is more complicated, and I elaborate on this point below.

Fundamentally, it is not a question of studying stratification from either the objective or the subjective perspective but of how the two approaches are complementary. My studies of the superordinate sectors of Mexican society indicate that one without the other is incomplete and gives a skewed notion of stratification. Rather than think about social class and mobility in terms of objective and subjective criteria, which unconsciously connote the former as more real than the latter, the appropriate strategy is to regard these criteria as entailing respectively structural and expressive variables and factors in intimate interaction. From this standpoint, one should establish the necessary conditions that enable one to isolate and conceptualize the meaningful, operational classes of a stratification system. The second step is to establish the expressive behaviors that accompany all social classes in the system, by themselves and in relationship to one another. It should be noted, however, that the initial observations that lead to the identification and definition of a class are almost invariably expressive. But why is it conceptually significant to keep separate the structural and expressive components of class?

The importance of the expressive components in classifying people into meaningful units was impressed on me by observing that the behavior of individuals was always more visible and immediate than the attribution of structural criteria that determines their status in the local society. In other words, objective criteria determine people's differential status in a social system, whereas the behavior exhibited in the roles they play is determined by subjective criteria. This is a universal characteristic of rank and class, and in the case of Mexico, it obtains as one moves from incipient stratification in rural folk communities to the superordinate sectors of society. A couple of examples should clarify the matter.

First, in transitional Mestizo communities, in which stratification is emerging, the first class to form is that of rich (by local standards) individuals (and families), the majority of whom, to validate their new standing, play an important role in the *cargo* (religious sponsorship) system. The ethnographer does not initially observe their new social and economic standing in the community but rather their behavior, say, as important stewards (mayordomos) and the manifold expressive activities that go with the role. On the basis of this observed behavior, one cannot determine that they are members of an incipient class; this must be done independently, and by elicitation, by establishing the economic affluence, marriage patterns, and other attributes that define the emerging class.

Second, at the other end of the spectrum, aristocrats and plutocrats in Mexico City are two different classes of the superordinate sector of the city but interact in many contexts and occasions. By exclusively observing the way they act and behave, it would be impossible to determine that plutocrats are virtually the ruling class of the country and that aristocrats are in their last stage as a social class. By virtue of a process of expressive acculturation that has been going on for more than two generations, plutocrats have learned to behave like aristocrats, but aristocrats have not learned to make money like plutocrats.

A third consideration for keeping expressive and structural variables and factors separate concerns the diachronic aspects of stratification, that is, the transformation and expressive survival of a class when it has lost most or all of its structural attributes. This is the case with all Western aristocracies, which, since the demise of the ancien régime, have ceased to be ruling classes and no longer have any significant power or wealth but still remain social classes eliciting recognition and embodying social exaltedness. More specifically, the Mexican aristocracy survives as a recognized social class of the superordinate sector of society after they lost all ruling functions after the 1910 Revolution. The aristocracy survived as the expressive model for the new plutocracy that began to emerge shortly after the end of the armed phase of the Revolution; the plutocracy is now the ruling class of the country.

With modifications and different implications, the same phenomenon obtains at a lower level in the stratificational scale, as I have observed it in several provincial cities of central Mexico. Puebla is a case in point. As a new plutocracy has come into existence, replacing the once rich and powerful aristocracy that after the Revolution lost everything and emigrated to Mexico City, traditional upper-middle-class families, which were the social support circle of the aristocracy, retain today a significant degree of social prominence and are sought by the new rich, though most of them are not affluent. Here again expressive considerations account for the survival of this social sector of the city, as structurally they have retained the same position they had when the aristocracy dominated social and economic life.

Finally, there is an aspect of expression that plays a crucial role in the study of stratification, particularly social mobility. This is what I have called elsewhere (Nutini 2004) vicarious expression. Very briefly, I use the term "vicariousness" to denote "the state experienced or realized through imaginative or sympathetic participation in the experience of another [person]" (*Webster's Third New International Dictionary* 1969). So defined, vicariousness is one of the most universal variations of natural expression, particularly associated with class stratification and mobility, and plays an important role in the dynamics of the most varied contexts of social interaction. Used collectively, as it is used in this book, vicarious expression means that upward mobility from one class to another entails the emulation of the expressive behavior of the higher class.

This aspect of stratification is dealt with in detail below; suffice to say here that without it, one cannot entirely understand social mobility.

THE EXPRESSIVE COMPONENTS OF CLASS AND MOBILITY: ENTAILMENTS AND IMPLICATIONS

In this section I discuss how, in what contexts, and to what extent expression complements the structural conceptualization of class and mobility. The main objective is to show that the so-called objective criteria do not by any means exhaust the description and analysis of class and, more specifically, that the motivation for social mobility is largely determined by expressive considerations. In fact, the role of expression in provincial class and mobility is placed in the comparative context of superordinate stratification: does expression entail the same consequences in these different milieus, and if not, what are the factors that account for the difference?

A Brief Outline of Expression as Related to Stratification

Expression, as an attribute of sociocultural systems, is a manifestation of the psychic unity of humankind; although it is present in different forms, it always fulfills essentially the same function. The concept is a reflection of the fact that, for whatever psychological reasons, the social life of humans inevitably contains nonutilitarian elements that shape the discharge of the social structure. Although expression obeys primarily psychological motivation, it is realized in concrete sociocultural settings, and its explanation therefore involves the confluence of psychological and sociological variables. It is the latter that is of primary significance here.

I do not mean to imply ontologically, that is, that the total ensemble of social action and cultural phenomena can be divided into patterns, activities, and domains that either have pragmatic value or represent ends in themselves. This is a false dichotomy. Epistemologically, though, it makes sense to distinguish between the utilitarian and nonutilitarian, because it forces one to determine the circumstances, contexts, and motivations that make behavior pragmatic or expressive. In the context of stratification, for example, the utilitarian, structural variables of economic affluence, education, and occupation do indeed constitute the necessary conditions for social mobility, but the immediate, sufficient motivation is invariably expressive. This is the crux of expressive analysis, that is, to account for the motivation behind any behavior or action that cannot be accounted for by the effect of structural variables. I am assuming, of course, that there are many kinds of behavior that cannot be understood or explained by structural or ideological variables alone. It goes without saying that if this premise is denied, then there is no such thing as expression: what is called expressive behavior is caused by specific material conditions, or the superstructures that these material conditions entail—ideology, values, worldview, and other ideational constructs. None of these constructs, however, can entirely account for how one chooses a profession, why groups with the same economic and social configuration have different behavioral styles, the strategies that people employ in the acquisition of power and wealth, and, directly related to stratification, why it is that some members of a social class are upwardly mobile whereas others are not. One of the main concerns of this book is to provide some answers to the last question.

The most difficult task in the analysis of expression is to isolate what is pragmatic and what is an end in itself in understanding or explaining cultural patterns, activities, and domains. The reason is that expression is at once contextual and contextually defined and created. Thus expression may take place in any domain of culture, contextualized by time and space. Equally true, however, expressive behavior is generated by specific historical circumstances of an economic, social, political, or religious nature. In other words, contextualized expression is a universal phenomenon manifested in varying sectors of culture.

Expression, as the concept is employed here, is an aspect of individual action but always in specific contexts. Though expressive behavior has a psychological component, its collective realization makes it a cultural construct. As such, expression is a construct in the same class as ideology, belief systems (values), and *imago mundi* but a distinct species. Unlike ideology, expression does not entail any efficacy, that is, moral constraints, imperatives to action, and value directives. Unlike a belief system, it does not generate any "thou shalls" or "thou shall nots"; and unlike the *imago mundi* of a social group, expression does not set the guidelines and parameters for interpreting the world. Expression and expressive behavior comprise those aspects of culture that are not grounded on or able to be concretized by material constraints, demographic considerations, and adaptations to natural environments. Given these premises, expression may be defined as a necessary component of culture that conditions behavior regardless of cultural content but contextualized in specific time and space. Specifying the conditions of time and space, then, becomes the cornerstone of expressive analysis. This operation permits us to establish the contextual realization of expression, that is, why a certain behavior or activity at times is utilitarian and at times non-utilitarian, and more important, it allows us to determine the consequences that follow from individual and collective action. To reiterate, expression is at once contextual and a contextually defined and created aspect of culture.

As far as class composition and mobility is concerned, sufficient expressive considerations constitute the contextual ambience of upward mobility, which is realized in the context of necessary structural variables that may vary from economic affluence and social position, training and education, and, at the lowest level, in the present context, to ethnic affiliation and distance to the Indian past. In other words, structural constraints constitute the necessary conditions for the sufficient efficacy of expressive variables in explaining the dynamics of mobility from one social class to another, for it is evident that not all members of a class have upward aspirations: some have, but probably the majority do not, beyond the natural proclivity to improve one's subsistence and material well-being. What I am asserting is that upward mobility is not entailed by individuals and groups simply taking advantage of structural factors (availability of work, opportunity of education, occasion to innovate, etc.) but by expressive constraints that either foster or impede the realization of this process. This is a theme that will recur in explaining class formation from the bottom to the top of the stratification system.

The structural dynamics of class formation are well understood, and they have been analyzed at length by sociologists (Bendix and Lipset 1966; Lopreato and Hazelrigg 1972; Wright 1985). Not so the expressive components of this equation, which have been discussed (Warner 1960; Baltzell 1966) but never well understood. Here the problem is centered on several aspects of the expressive array of social classes, particularly those concerning the exclusive and inclusive array. I have discussed in detail these aspects of expression elsewhere (Nutini 1988, 1995). Here I will confine myself to the essentials in order to make the ensuing discussion intelligible.

I define the expressive array as the total of all patterns or domains in a given social class that entirely or partially realize expression. Every social class in a stratification system has an expressive array that is peculiar to itself, in terms of both intensity and the domains in which expression is realized. Despite the absence of a working theory of expression and without the benefit of systematic, cross-cultural data, I have nonetheless established the following generalizations, based on my ethnographic knowledge of Araucanian society (tribal), rural Tlaxcalan society (folk), and Mexican aristocratic society (urban).

First, although every expressive array entails a unique organization of domains, and no two arrays are exactly alike, total content and form overlap significantly. One of the most characteristic attributes of the expressive array is that global content and form, as well as the content and form of specific domains, is shared by several social systems. For example, the expressive array of Italians, French, Spaniards, English, Germans, perhaps even Americans and Australians, manifest a degree of content and form that is exclusively their own while sharing the bulk of the array with Western society as a whole. Closer to the subject here, the same obtains in comparing the expressive array of rural Tlaxcalans with those of rural Oaxacans, Yucatecans, Pueblans, Guatemalans, and other folk societies of Mesoamerica. Can one say anything meaningful about the proportion of exclusive and inclusive content and form of expressive arrays? The answer is a tentative yes. I have established that the expressive array of any social group is about 20 percent exclusive in content and form, while 80 percent is shared with varying numbers of other social groups. In other words, 20 percent of the expressive array of rural Tlaxcalans is exclusively their own, while 80 percent of it is shared with all other folk societies in Mesoamerica.

Second, concentrating on class, in terms of expressive culture and behavior, this social category is probably the most salient and effective social sorter. Class appears always to have been the most efficacious compound variable in generating different expressive arrays, both within a single cultural tradition and across several, sometimes quite different, cultural traditions. That is, the expressive arrays of equivalent social classes generally reflect more similarities across subcultures, and not infrequently even across different cultural traditions, than they do across classes within the same subculture. Given certain social, economic, industrial, and commercial constraints and the efficient networks of communication and diffusion in the world today, one could speak of the expressive array of the rich and powerful, of international business and political bureaucracies, of diplomats, or even of so-called jet-setters. Likewise, the expressive arrays of the middle and lower classes cut across all of Western society, perhaps even of the world, again due to the homogenizing effects of industrialization and the diffusion of other Western complexes. The Mexican aristocracy displays an expressive array, for example, that resembles more closely the expressive array of the Spanish and Italian aristocracy than that of, say, Mexican plutocrats or upper middle classes, despite the fact that inclusively the aristocracy shares most of its expressive domains in varying proportions with the entire Mexican stratification system, from its rural Indian sector to its upper sectors in Mexico City. The inclusive bulk of content and form of expressive arrays, then, is much more culturally and subculturally bound. If one takes the expressive array of Mexican aristocrats, the exclusive core is most of the content and form of that 20 percent identified above; the remaining 80 percent is shared in varying proportions with all other classes in the Mexican stratification system, for they have the same religion, are bound by many social customs, and are constrained by the same political, environmental, and ecological variables. But that 20 percent is what distinguishes Mexican aristocrats as an expressive class from all other classes in Mexican society and secures their membership in the larger class of Western aristocrats.[1]

Third, though the main contexts of expression are the nonutilitarian aspects of culture, any aspect of culture may realize expressive behavior, regardless of manifestly utilitarian attributes and functions. No significant aspect of culture lacks potential expressive coloration. Just as cultures organize around contexts and themes that exceed the exigencies of subsistence and shelter, so the expressive array organizes around characteristic contexts and themes. In addition to the universal contexts of art and play, an expressive array derives its characteristic configuration and flavor from the contextual loci of its realization. Sports, dress, and etiquette, for example, are important loci of expressive behavior in Western culture, whereas in many tribal societies, ritual, certain aspects of religion, and oral tradition seem to be the main loci. More specifically, and closely related to this study, the inclusive expressive array of Mexican society is focused mainly on religious ritualism, devotional activities, kinship and compadrazgo, family life, and interpersonal relations.

At this point, we may ask, how are these expressive strands significant in analyzing class formation and mobility, and how will they be employed to generate understanding of stratification? I have tested a number of expressive hypotheses in the context of the superordinate stratification of Mexico (the social, ruling, and political classes of the country mostly enfranchised in Mexico City), and this study's central concern, beyond its descriptive dimensions, is to do the same in provincial stratification, with an emphasis on lower and middle sectors. I shall therefore briefly specify the main expressive variables and principles, as derived from the foregoing discussion, and the consequences they entail for class formation and mobility.

The Efficacy and Form of Substantive Expressive Variables

(1)

With respect to the inclusive array, it is important to have a clear picture of what social classes share, how what they share facilitates or impedes upward mobility, and the form in which the inclusive array shapes the expressive and structural configuration of classes. This is essentially a descriptive integrational task that provides substance and content to the mere structural description of classes. With respect to the exclusive array, the task is essentially analytic, as this array provides the contextual variables that establish collective motivation for upward mobility. To put it differently, the exclusive array determines the dynamic of upward mobility, that is, it is the activation and discharge of specific domains that propels individuals to emulate the expressive behavior and lifestyle of a higher class. Those individuals who do not pursue this strategy are by definition not upwardly mobile, even when they achieve better economic, material conditions than is the norm in the class they come from. From this standpoint, improving one's lot structurally (i.e., getting a better job, better housing, access to training and education, etc.) is only part of what constitutes upward mobility; acquiring the diagnostic, most salient domains of a higher class's expressive array completes the passage from one class to another, which is usually accompanied by increasing class consciousness.

I am asserting, in fact, that as individuals move from the lower to higher sectors of the stratification system, class consciousness increases, and this is one of the hypotheses that I expect to prove in this book. Thus, as people make the transition from folk (Indian and rural Mestizo populations) to urban working-class status and as they rise in the stratification scale from lower to higher class affiliation, the analysis of exclusive expressive domains provides significant inputs for explaining individual and collective mobility and how a new realignment of classes is taking place. In other words, isolating the expressive domains and entailing them to accompanying structural changes as people move from one class to another will explain the emerging stratification system: the rate of upward mobility, the form and content that each class is acquiring, the degree of class consciousness, and so on.

(2)

Closely related to the foregoing variable is the form and extent of expressive vicariousness, or, if you will, learning the ways of the superordinately placed (i.e., that of the class to which individuals aspire, almost invariably the one immediately above). Expressive emulation plays a determinant role in class formation and mobility; I positively tested this hypothesis in the study of the aristocracy and plutocracy enfranchised in Mexico City (Nutini 2004), and I expect to do the same along the entire spectrum of provincial stratification. In the case of the former, plutocrats emulate aristocrats in the process of becoming the highest social class of the city, and emulation takes place primarily in the contexts of etiquette and demeanor, personal attire, household decoration and display, and entertainment, in addition to other domains associated with social exaltedness. In the case of the latter, emulation takes place in essentially the same manner, and what varies is the intensity of emulation and the domains that are emulated. How and in what degrees does expressive emulation take place in provincial stratification?

With respect to the intensity of expressive emulation, it increases as individuals move from the bottom to the top of the stratification scale. For example, the transition from middle class to upper middle class includes more domains (more diversified contexts of expression) than the transition from rural folk to urban working class. With respect to what is being emulated, this changes from material and subsistence domains to increasingly nonmaterial and ideational-sumptuary domains of behavior. For example, housing, dress, and technology are the domains that mark the passage from rural folk to urban working class, whereas the emulation of personal demeanor, exhibition, and display characterize the transition from middle-class to upper-middle-class or elite status. Of course, a global understanding of expressive emulation, as people move from the bottom to the top of the stratification scale, is crucial to determining the principles that underlie a realignment of classes that has not yet run its course.

(3)

The third consideration is not so much a variable as a statement on the sufficient efficacy of expression in the study of stratification. Granting that power and wealth (the main objective factors), or lack thereof, structure, configure, and set the parameters of the expressive culture of all social classes, it is nonetheless the case that though class consciousness, class recognition, and class composition are determined by the possession of wealth and power, the perception of class, its visibility, and its place in the social system are provided by its social and expressive behavior. What is observed, internalized, and made into the ostensible definition of a class by the members of all other classes in the stratification system is the product of objective conditions but modified, in feedback fashion, by historical circumstances and the nonutilitarian choices allowed by the expressive array. The visibility—pervasive gestalt, one might say—of class perception is the most distinct and universal characteristic of class. It defines its entire range of social relations with the other classes of the stratification system. Visibility here denotes not only that the exclusive expressive array of a class is its most immediately and globally perceived attribute but also that its perception entails the most desirable quality for upward mobility.

Most concepts of class maintain that stratification is a social phenomenon that arises in complex societies either from certain specific cultural ensembles that require a social division of labor or from the unequal distribution of and access to resources. To explain a class from this standpoint, one makes a historical assessment of economic, political, religious, and other variables and places them in synchronic interaction. This approach leaves unexplained, however, motivation and certain inherent aspects of stratification; here the expressive analysis of class is most useful. For example, in the long evolution of Western stratification, from classical times to the present, every new stage in the rearrangement of classes has been characterized by a fairly distinct expressive array. On a small scale, this is exemplified here in the context of class formation and mobility and the realignment of classes that has taken place during the past two generations.

Expressive Principles and the Structure of Stratification

(1)

The well-known Mexican saying, "Juntos pero no revueltos" is a principle (perhaps diagnostic-guideline-to-action is a better term) that applies from top to bottom of the Mexican stratification system but is more stringently efficacious in the higher rungs. The Mexican stratification system is at the same time quite closed and quite open. This is another way of saying that, while upward class mobility is not nearly as fluid as, say, in the United States, social interaction among the classes is significantly fluid. From a slightly different perspective, the fluidity of social interaction in Mexican society stems from the fact that class barriers are much more difficult to breach than in U.S. society: in the former, the security and distinctness of class membership permits social interaction without loss of status; in the latter, the impermanence and blurred boundaries of class do not allow for such free social interaction, and barriers are set up behaviorally to ward off loss of status.[2]

(2)

The expressive dimensions generated by the encompassing domains of race and ethnicity are another important variable in assessing class formation and mobility. On the surface it would appear that these domains, so relatively straightforward and unchangeable, would not entail any significant expressive components. Quite the contrary, they are pregnant with expressive attributes and entailments, as I have ascertained in the superordinate context of Mexico City—even more so in the context of provincial stratification, where there is much greater ethnic-phenotypic variation. Physical type, presentation of the self, and enhancing or playing down physical and cultural traits are important in self-definition and identification by others. Individuals cannot fundamentally alter their physical presence, but they can certainly present themselves socially and culturally so as to enhance certain traits or divert attention from others. In this ambience, the manipulation of phenotypical traits acquires expressive significance and colors many aspects of social class and mobility. I have investigated this phenomenon in the superordinate context of Mexico City and the folk context of the Tlaxcala-Pueblan Valley, which in the present context needs to be elaborated.

The manipulation of phenotypic traits, and cultural interpretation of them, is a juncture that is accurately denoted by the folk wisdom of the saying, "La gente se emblanquece a medida que hacen dinero" (People become whitened to the extent that they acquire wealth [which in this context implies rising on the social scale]).[3] I call this "the whitening syndrome," a rich, expression-generating context that encompasses a great deal of behavioral interaction, which is realized differentially at all levels of Mexican society. The potency of this expression-generating context stems from the fact that in Mexican society as a whole the standards of beauty and phenotypical desirability are European. From Indians to aristocrats, Mexicans view people through the prism of Caucasoid phe-notypical ensembles and act so as to maximize specific ends: social class advancement, economic advantage, and even political and religious goals. In this ambience, utilitarian behavior and action invariably have an expressive coloration or outright expressive component: what varies from class to class is the configuration of expressive domains and subdo-mains that accompany utilitarian behavior and action in the pursuit of specific goals.

I want to make clear that what I have called the whitening syndrome has rather long antecedents among anthropologists working in Latin Amer-ica. It is not certain who was the first to have identified the syndrome, but at least fifty years ago it was hinted at or overtly discussed by the anthro-pologists Gillin (1945), Beals (1954), Tumin (1962), and Wagley (1965) and, shortly thereafter, Harris (1964), Palerm (1972); more recently, Friedlander (1975), Ariel de Vidas (1994), and Levine (1997) have done the same. These anthropologists understood that everywhere, but partic-ularly in Latin America, the phenotypic and somatic components of race are to a significant extent cultural constructs that people manipulate in various ways for political, economic, and social aims. In a variety of con-texts and with slight variations, the whitening syndrome has been em-ployed in the analysis of social class and mobility, especially in countries such as Mexico that have a high Amerindian racial component and in which the manipulation of somatic and phenotypic traits is the highest.

How is this expression-generating context realized in the various strata of Mexican society? There are two aspects to this question: indi-vidual and collective self-perception and how individuals and classes are exogenously perceived. Several examples should make this clear, as we go from the top to the bottom of the stratification system, from the su-perordinate stratification in Mexico City to all the classes of provincial stratification.

First, the aristocracy in Mexico City perceives itself as phenotypically European, and, all things being equal, individual aristocrats extend so-cial recognition to others in terms of somatic appearance, namely, to plu-tocrats and members of the upper middle class who are regarded as akin to them. From this viewpoint, then, the superordinately placed are "so-cially" regarded as phenotypically European. In this context, expressive manipulation takes place, and individuals who exhibit somatic traits that deviate from the phenotypical standards of aristocrats tend to be mini-mized, that is, are "whitened" and made more appealing. This is the generalized syndrome that applies to three of the sectors (the aristocracy, the plutocracy, and the political class) of the superordinate class. The political class does not fit this sociophenotypical characterization, for its perceived composition ranges from Indian to European but is stereotyped as an essentially Mestizo sector beyond the *tolerable* phenotypical manipulation of "white" aristocrats, plutocrats, and the upper middle class. The superordinate class as a whole, however, is perceived by the majority of the subordinately placed as the "whitest" sector of society, by virtue of the power and wealth it denotes. This position in society, according to the ideology of race and ethnicity, commands, all things being equal, more honor and respect than are accorded to the common citizen. It should be noted that, though this still subservient attitude is changing rapidly, it attests to the persistence of signeurial traits. Taking into consideration the differences of wealth, sophistication, and degree of elaboration that characterize provincial stratification, essentially the same obtains in the superordinate sector of Córdoba and surrounding region (see Chapter 3).

Second, in the middle strata of society (the middle and working classes) the same situation obtains but with significantly more fluidity. In this vast spectrum, it is not so much the striving for social recognition that leads people to manipulate somatic appearance (namely, to enhance European phenotypic traits or "whiten" individuals for social gain) but rather making conscious decisions and taking specific actions that would redound in bringing individuals and groups (families, kinsmen, and networks of friends) closer to the European standards of beauty and appearance that Mexican society imposes. The self-perception/being perceived contrast also obtains but with greater emphasis on being perceived by others as a means to an end, not necessarily for social advancement, but for specific economic gain, and always constrained by the ideological standards of Caucasoid somatology. The ostensible model that, to a significant extent, guides the behavior and action of individuals and groups in this middle strata is omnipresent and manifested in many "cultural" and communication environments: advertising, television, cinema, and even the graphic arts. In this general ambience of exogenous, imperialist ideology of color, somatic characteristics and standards of beauty, middle-class individuals and groups engage in many expressive behaviors. This is perhaps the most noxious aspect of the colonial inheritance, which by now, of course, is an integral part of the social and cultural fabric of the nation.

Briefly, the manipulation of phenotypes to enhance the connotation of European traits, or to increase other people's perception of individuals and groups as more European, may henceforth be encapsulated as "the cultural whitening syndrome." [4] What is the realization of this syndrome in the middle strata of Mexican society, and what are its consequences? Primarily, the syndrome is an ideological guide to action that fosters the maximization of European traits or, conversely, makes less noticeable the presence of Indian-Mestizo traits. Thus the generated expressive behavior is centered on personal physical presentation and the conscious desire to demonstrate European ancestry.

As I discuss in chapters 4 and 5, the generated behavior ranges from women not shaving their legs to men and women avoiding apparel and usages betraying Indian-Mestizo origins. The syndrome is realized at all levels of the middle strata but is probably more pronounced among solid middle-class individuals and groups, where it acquires an element of upward mobility, namely, the desire to be enhanced socially after a level of economic affluence has been achieved. Secondarily, and with the most generalized incidence in the upper rungs of the middle strata of society, are practices that aim to "improve" one's phenotypical appearance, or to be perceived as more Caucasoid, either immediately or for the benefit of one's progeny. This is achieved expressively by association with individuals who are closer to the ideal standards of physical appearance, which frequently entails preferential behavior and undue respect to them, even when they may be poorer or have less power. This, of course, is characteristic of the upwardly mobile, whereas the majority of individuals in the middle of the stratification pyramid pay only lip service to the ideology of physical appearance and comportment. The middle strata of the stratification system (self-perceived and perceived by the majority of Mexican society as Mestizo and hence a phenotypically mixed population) manifest the cultural whitening syndrome as a function of somatic-cultural upward aspirations in the game of approaching the ideal standards of somatic appearance. In other words, the middle rungs of the stratification system are constrained by the dominant ideology of the whitening syndrome by taking advantage of it, without which economic and social ends-in-view would be more difficult to achieve.

Third, at the bottom strata of Mexican society (the rural and urban poor and the transitional and traditional Indian population), the cultural whitening syndrome is also significantly realized. The vast majority of Mexicans composing this strata are perceived by themselves and by the rest of society as phenotypically undifferentiated, as there is often no or slight somatic discrimination between Indians and Mestizos. Distinctions are essentially cultural, even when at the local or regional level people use terminology that may denote racial characteristics (Indians refer to non-Indians as white, *güero*, and several other racially loaded terms, and Mestizos refer to Indians as *indígenas, inditos,* and other equally racially loaded terms). In most areas of the country where there are large numbers of Indians, given that phenotypical differences between Indians and Mestizos are usually either nonexistent or difficult to pinpoint (by individuals and groups culturally defined as Indians and Mestizos), does somatic discrimination (distinction) take place? The answer is yes but blurred by cultural considerations. For example, in regions where a rather strong cultural dichotomy obtains between these two groups, individuals and groups discriminate between Mestizo and Caucasian phenotypes but almost invariably ethnically bound: Indians refer to non-Mestizo individuals as *catrines, gente blanca,* and other local terms, whereas Mestizos refer to them as gringos or *extranjeros,* or by nationality or ethnic qualifiers. Although Indian and Mestizo categories of self-definition and perception are culturally bound, Indians and Mestizos quite clearly recognize phenotypic differences beyond the somatic common denominator that binds them as a racial group. In this environment, then, both Indians and Mestizos manifest the cultural whitening syndrome in a limited fashion, as falling within the orbit of influence of the syndrome's powerful ideology: Indians in the passage to Mestizo status, rural Mestizos when they migrate to the city.

Much the same obtains in urban environments, with the significant difference that the syndrome at this level is found mostly among Mestizos vying for specific economic ends or aspiring to upward social mobility. The ideology of the cultural whitening syndrome compels the lowest, most numerous sectors of the stratification system to engage in the physical and symbolic manipulation of phenotypic traits, self-directed or other-directed: self-directed, in unconsciously behaving in certain ways so as to bridge the somatic gap between phenotypic perceptions and ideologic imperatives; other-directed, in consciously acting or making decisions that will affect the way in which individuals and groups are perceived by those who in one way or another are above their stations. As in the case of the top and middle strata of society, the cultural whitening syndrome generates a complex of domains and subdomains that significantly enriches the expressive culture of the majority of Mexican society. (See chapters 4 and 5 for a fuller discussion.)

To summarize, the ideology of the cultural whitening syndrome is a powerful generator of expressive realization at all levels of Mexican society. It cuts across race, class, and ethnicity and configures many expressive domains in the social, economic, political, and even religious life of the manifold rungs of the stratification system. This is a good example of ideological imperialism, so much a part of the national culture that it has become second nature to the overwhelming majority of Mexicans. It perpetuates a large body of expression that probably not even the most drastic transformation of society can eradicate completely.

(3)

Not directly related to race and somatology but very much a part of class and ethnicity is the heightened sense of exclusivity and the restricted consciousness of kind that characterize Mexican society. These characteristics translate into guides to action that have important implications for understanding class formation and mobility as well as the transition from one ethnic group to another. Together with the foregoing variables, this syndrome explains much of the dynamics of stratification and the new realignment of classes that has been taking place since the Revolution of 1910. The combined effect of these principles, or guides to action, demonstrates how much the stratification system of Mexico has changed and at the same time retained some of its traditional characteristics: the system has become significantly more open and fluid, while persistent constraining factors render it different from the system of Western industrial nations with longer democratic traditions. Exclusivity and consciousness of kind affects the superordinate and subordinate (the middle and bottom) sectors of the stratification system in two ways. The first affects only the superordinate sector, and it concerns expressive acculturation and the emergence of a new ruling class. The second affects both sectors, and it has to do with the restrictiveness of interpersonal categories that has serious consequences for the creation of citizenship.

When I say that the stratification system in particular and Mexican society in general are characterized by exclusivity and a group-endogenous consciousness of kind, I mean to convey the fragmentation of a pluriethnic country composed not only of many ethnicities but also of separate social groups that have not entirely coalesced into a distinct nationality. The Revolution was, of course, a crucial step forward, but Mexican society still exhibits colonial traits that have conspired against its maturation as a national state. In no domain of culture is this fragmentation more apparent than in social relations, class-consciousness, and the process of nation building. Indeed, the concept of citizenship in Mexico is weak and does not transcend the community, or at best the region.

Fundamentally, most people in Mexico, in different degrees and from top to bottom in the stratification system, recognize and are constrained (have rights and obligations) by the following categories of people: kinsmen, ritual kinsmen, friends, and neighbors. Beyond the realm of action and behavior of these categories, there are no effective social categories that regulate and control the social life of Mexicans. This, of course, is another way of saying that the category of citizen and the institution of citizenship are weak, and some segments of the population lack them altogether. In the environment of kinship, compadrazgo, friendship, and neighborhood, the social life of the people at all levels of social integration is generally smooth, redounds in well-structured groups and networks, and seldom entails irreconcilable predicaments. But in terms of citizenship, in the context of the wider world, the situation changes rather dramatically: disorganization abounds, there is little respect for laws and regulations, and consideration for the rights of others is minimal and usually enforced by immediate retribution. It is beyond the scope of this book to even outline the manifold manifestations of exclusivity and lack of consciousness of being a citizen and what they entail behaviorally. Perhaps an example will make clear what this means in the lowest rungs of the stratification system, as a basis for outlining briefly what transpires as we ascend the social scale.

In Indian and the majority of traditional rural Mestizo communities, kinship, compadrazgo, friendship, and neighborhood are the fundamental institutions that configure the social life of the people. These institutions are sufficient to structure an orderly, smooth-functioning society in which the rights of others are respected, there is collective responsibility, and duties and obligations are adequately discharged. You can thus speak of a highly developed sense of "citizenship" that is determined by both the small and circumscribed nature of the local group and the "sacralized" nature of social relations. When communities become secularized by the process of rapid growth and in time are transformed and become part of the national world, this "sacralized form of citizenship" begins to decline. Moreover, when individuals leave the community and settle permanently in the city, they bring with them the same social categories that efficiently organize the traditional village. In other words, integration into the national framework, collectively and individually, entails the continuation of kinship, compadrazgo, friendship, and neighborhood as the only recognized categories that structure orderly social life. I interpret this as a form of exclusivity that generates a consciousness of kind within the group that these institutions condition, which tend to exclude most behavioral responsibility beyond their confines. Evidently, these categories are insufficient to structure orderly social life in the larger context of the nation. Thus the citizenship that is necessary for the proper functioning of a nation is never developed and disorganization becomes the norm. Everything beyond the sphere of influence of these institutions does not seem to have the same importance, and, hence, there is disregard for the institutions, rules, and obligations that bind the body politic of the nation. In a nutshell, the folk institutions of Indians and rural Mestizos do not successfully make the transition to the cultural context of the nation: socialized in the protective, demographically circumscribed ambience of the community, citizenship is never sufficiently developed in the greater society; this is an adaptive situation that only now is slowly beginning to change.[5]

In the middle rungs of the stratification system, exclusivity and consciousness of kind have basically the same functional constitution described above, except that they are differently manifested. Sacralized, folk citizenship does not obtain in the same efficacious communal fashion, as kinship declines and compadrazgo acquires a significant vertical, patron-client component. What survives of the folk ambience is the continuous reliance on these two institutions but in a reduced form and with greater emphasis on friendship and neighborhood. The net result, however, is essentially not different as it obtains in the transition from folk to national life. Middle- and lower-middle-class culture is centered on the ambience of the aforementioned institutions. Consciousness of a clear notion of citizenship is still weak and does not structure behavior and social relations in the impersonal domains of the nation. Another way of putting it is that the great majority of Mexicans have a keen sense of personal duty and responsibility but a weak sense of impersonal, abstract rights and obligations to fellow citizens. However, education is making a difference and citizenship is increasingly asserting itself. This is particularly the situation in the case of disaster. For example, during the 1985 earthquake that profoundly affected central Mexico, the population of Mexico City behaved according to the best standards of citizenship anywhere.

Briefly, since it is only tangentially related to the main thrust of this work, at the top of the stratification system exclusivity and consciousness of kind take the classical form of superordinate stratification; particularly after the demise of the estate system, the upper classes have exhibited the highest degree of exclusivity and class endogeny. Suffice it to say here that the three sectors of the superordinate class, despite being the most educated segment of the population (with the exception of rather small intellectual groups of the middle classes), have not developed an adequate consciousness of citizenship and are not basically different in this respect from the middle and bottom sectors of the stratification system. The aristocracy, plutocracy, and upper middle class are the most self-contained rungs of society, and each in its own sphere of interaction is as isolated from the rest of society as Indian and Mestizo communities.

To conclude, of all the variables discussed in this section, the cultural whitening syndrome is the most encompassing, and, with slight variations, as people ascend the social scale from Indian to haute bourgeois, the syndrome remains the same: the more European an individual looks at the top, and concomitantly, the less Indian an individual looks in the middle and lower rungs of society, the more it helps one to succeed and achieve social, economic, and perhaps even political goals. The basic phenotypical principle has multiple variations that enhance, impede, or smooth social mobility and govern many domains of social interaction. While one could say that Mexican society is as racist as U.S. society, the cultural manipulation of phenotypes makes the former more humane and less destructive than the latter. This fundamental aspect of Mexican social interaction is the result of the cultural imperialism of a colonial past that has permanently marked the life of the nation by imposing standards of beauty, appearance, and behavior that are essentially European.[6]

THE STRUCTURAL, OBJECTIVE COMPONENTS OF STRATIFICATION: ORGANIZATION OF THE DESCRIPTION AND ANALYSIS

Sociologists have dealt extensively with the structural aspects of stratification. Therefore, this section presents a brief discussion of how a traditional monograph on class and mobility is structured. It specifies how the ensuing chapters present the expressive and structural data as they interrelate at several key junctures. In addition, I discuss the modus operandi that underlies the description and analysis of this book in relation to the main parameters of class differentiation, expressive elaboration, and context of realization.

After placing the city of Córdoba and surrounding region in historical, demographic, and geographic perspective (Chapter 2), I describe and analyze each of the main stratification sectors of society, and their subdivisions: the ruling, superordinate class of industrialists, businessmen, and politicians (Chapter 3); the middle classes of merchants, farmers, and professionals and the working classes of factory and white-collar workers (Chapter 4); and the urban dispossessed and rural folk (Chapter 5). In the conclusion, I present an assessment of studying stratification by the combined structural-expressive approach and some generalizations on class consciousness and mobility.

Each chapter first describes and analyzes the structural composition of the class: its social ranking, economic wealth or lack thereof, material culture, political participation, and religious practices. Since the classes, as specified above, are composed of two or three quite distinct "subclasses," it is necessary to specify other objective variables, such as education, occupation, place of residence, and so on, that characterize them. Moreover, each class entails different combinations of objective traits that must be assessed to establish the differential attributes of mobility as people move from one class to another. For example, in the case of the passage from rural folk and urban dispossessed to working class, place of residence and education are hardly significant, whereas acquiring material well-being, particularly a better house and some essential technological implements such as a kitchen stove and a television set, constitutes a definite indication of having acquired the status of the gainfully employed. By contrast, in the move from middle-class to upper-middle-class status, place of residence is essential, and, while education may or may not be significant, material acquisitions are usually nonessential luxury items such as fine furniture, artwork, and the like. These examples suggest that as people move from the bottom to the top of the stratificational scale, the items that are acquired in the transition from one class to another entail increasingly expressive behavior.

Second, class formation, roughly since 1940, is a central concern. It is possible to reconstruct fairly well what the stratification system of Córdoba and the region was in 1940, that is, at the end of President Cárdenas's massive land reform. This coincides with the demise of the hacienda system in the region and the end of the influence of hacendados in the city. This is a key event in the development of regional stratification that initiates the realignment of classes that has not yet run its course. Chapters 3 through 5 describe the transformation undergone by the five broad classes that putatively constitute the regional stratification system; in the conclusion and throughout the text a global analysis of class mobility entailed by economic, demographic, political, and other factors is presented.

Third, class mobility is of course a concomitant aspect of class formation, but I have deemed it best to treat it separately. The main reason for taking this analytical stand is that, more than any aspect of stratification, mobility entails expressive components. To reiterate, class mobility is basically determined by the sufficient effect of expressive motivation and emulation, as they are realized in the necessary structural context of the economic, demographic, and political factors of the past two and a half generations. From a slightly different perspective, the structural conditions provide the milieu in which expressive choices are realized and class mobility is given ostensible form and perceived by other social classes. Based on these considerations, special care is taken to isolate the expressive factors that are directly and indirectly entailed in structural variables.

Fourth, class consciousness, which is also related to class formation and mobility, needs to be handled separately because it involves structural and expressive components but at different levels of realization. On the one hand, structural class consciousness entails collective awareness and self-perception and group action in various domains having to do with improving the general well-being of the class. This means basically that classes must be analyzed in the context of the entire stratification system in order to determine interclass relationships (which, in a pluriethnic society such as Mexico, are invariably affected by ethnicity and phenotypical appearance) and gauge the rate and nature of mobility. On the other hand, expressive class consciousness entails individual awareness and being exogenously perceived as sharing patterns of behavior and action that distinguish the class from all others in the system. Moreover, expressive class consciousness is directly related to motivating people to vicarious emulation, and it is therefore necessary to establish the individual factors that induce and shape the process of acquiring the material, behavioral, and attitudinal traits of another class. One might say that assessing the degree of consciousness of a social class consists essentially in isolating the structural-collective and expressive-individual factors and how they synergistically affect class formation and mobility.

To reiterate, the basic assumption of this book is that structural variables by themselves do not account for class formation and mobility and that expressive factors modify, enhance, or inhibit structural factors in various cultural domains. Therefore, in the description and analysis of the stratification system of Córdoba and surrounding region, the emphasis is on identifying junctures and occasions in which structural and expressive variables and factors are efficaciously entailed.

There is no model for presenting the expressive components of class, or for placing them in relation to other classes of the stratification system.

Inasmuch as these points are discussed in the conclusion, suffice it to say here that the general modus operandi guiding my description and analysis is based on the proposition that it is best to present the expressive ethnography of stratification after a structural ethnography has been generated. Thus the discussion of all aspects and domains of the structural configuration (from material culture and wealth to politics and religion) and ideational domains (class consciousness, manners and mores, etc.) of all classes of the stratification system is accompanied by individual expressive analyses. This methodological approach, which I employed in the study of the aristocracy and plutocracy in Mexico City, entails optimal conditions for the implementation of the study of stratification as envisaged in this book.

In this chapter, I have put in perspective the structural and expressive elements of the analytical approach and the methodological techniques underlying this study. My intention has been to present a gestalt of what to expect in the description and analysis, leading to the clarification of concepts and the standardization of procedures. This is a necessary step, given that there are no previous studies of stratification in which expressive components constitute the sufficient condition for the understanding and explanation of social class and mobility.

| CÓRDOBA AND ITS ENVIRONS

*Historical, Demographic, and
Geographic Considerations*

The city of Córdoba is located in the temperate zone (tierra templada) in the state of Veracruz on the eastern slopes of the Sierra Madre Oriental. Together with the city of Orizaba, ten miles away, it faces Citlalteptl, an extinct volcano, also known as Pico de Orizaba, that is the second highest mountain in North America. Located on the main Mexico City–Veracruz highway and approximately seventy-five miles from the city of Veracruz, Córdoba is the market town for a large, rich agricultural area that extends from the small city of Coscomatepec in the north to the city of Zongolica in the south and from the town of Ixhuatlan in the west to the city of Cuitlahuac in the east. This agricultural area includes many villages and towns and five small cities—Coscomatepec, population 20,000; Fortin de las Flores, 25,000; Cuitlahuac, 40,000; Yanga, 30,000; and Zongolica, 20,000—with a total population of about 850,000 (XII Censo General de Población 2001). The stratification system described and analyzed here applies to the entire region.

HISTORICAL OUTLINE OF THE CITY AND THE REGION

Córdoba was founded in 1618, but the region has been agriculturally important since the beginning of the colonial period. Sugarcane was introduced soon after the Spanish conquest and became the main commercial crop of the region. In 1800 coffee was introduced. Since then, coffee and sugarcane have been the pillars of the regional economy (Rodríguez y Valero 1756; Belmonte Guzmán 1987). The region's fertile land also produces many staple crops.

In pre-Hispanic times, the region was sparsely populated by Totonac and Nahuatl Indians (who, during the two generations preceding the

Spanish conquest, had migrated from the Tlaxcala-Pueblan Valley), which resulted in the granting of few *encomiendas*. This demographic fact led to the importation of a large number of black slaves who throughout the nineteenth century were absorbed into the local Indian and Mestizo population. This black racial strain can be seen in the phenotypic composition of the population of the region today. Blacks, however, no longer constitute an independent ethnic group, as the last entirely black communities disappeared during the past two generations (Dyfrig McH. Forbes pers. com. 1976).

The city was established on the Lomas de Huilango by thirty Spanish settlers (vecinos) from several towns and cities of central Mexico but primarily from the nearby towns of Huatusco, Orizaba, and Coscomatepec (Cabral Pérez 1998). The city was named after Diego Fernández de Córdoba, the thirteenth viceroy of New Spain, who secured the royal grant for the foundation of the town (*villa*). That the vecinos of the newly founded town were made *hidalgos* (gentry) gave rise to the legend that the city was founded by thirty knights (*treinta caballeros*). The town was established to safeguard the commerce between Veracruz and Mexico City against runaway black slaves (*negros cimarrones*) and assorted bandits who preyed on the region (Luna de Carpinteyro 1991).

The city prospered throughout the seventeenth century and rapidly became the economic center of the region. By the last decade of the century, the town boasted several impressive edifices, including two of the arcades (*portales,* structures that still exhibit their original architectural features, surrounding the *zócalo,* or main square), the parochial church, and at least six other churches. Córdoba had become an urbanized, bustling commercial center with more than fifteen thousand inhabitants (Andrade 1966).

By the end of the colonial period, the civic center of the city had become essentially what it is today: a prosperous urban center with more than twenty thousand inhabitants. In 1821 two events took place in Córdoba and its environs of which its inhabitants today are extremely proud. On May 21, Mexican insurgents, with the participation of many Cordobeses, defeated the royal forces in a decisive battle for independence; and on August 24, the Tratado de Córdoba was signed in the city, formally recognizing the "Imperio Mexicano" as a sovereign state. The treaty was signed by Juan O'Donojú, the last viceroy of New Spain, who had recently arrived in Veracruz, and Agustín de Iturbide, the self-proclaimed "emperor" of Mexico (Andrade 1966).

In 1830 the town of Córdoba was promoted to the demographic status of a city. This was the high point in the history of Córdoba, and for nearly a century, until the Mexican Revolution of 1910, Córdoba languished under the shadow of Orizaba, where most of the commerce and industry of west-central Veracruz was concentrated. Nonetheless, a few industries—primarily processing plants—flourished in Córdoba, as this part of the state entered the machine age. More significantly, Córdoba became an important educational center, rivaling Xalapa (the capital of the state) and Veracruz (its largest city). Between independence and mid-century, five colleges were founded, one for women (an uncommon occurrence in Mexico at that time), and Córdoba remained an important intellectual center until the presidency of Lázaro Cárdenas (1934–1940). From then on, due to the preeminence of state and federal educational institutions (universities, colleges, technical schools, and high schools), Córdoba was left behind, as the most prestigious educational institutions were sited in Jalapa, Veracruz, and Orizaba (Arriola Molina 1983).

The population of Córdoba remained constant until the turn of the century, when it slowly began to grow. By 1919 the city had a population of about 35,000. From then on it began to grow at a rapid pace, and by 1980 it had more than 250,000 inhabitants. Today, Córdoba's population approaches 456,000. As the city grew, it began to attract industry and became a diversified commercial and transportation center. It surpassed Orizaba, and after Veracruz and Xalapa, it is the most important commercial and transportation city in the state (Herrera Moreno 1987).

Between 1916 and 1920, Córdoba became the capital of the state of Veracruz. The reasons for this are not entirely clear; they had to do with the political dislocation that accompanied the last three years of the armed phase of the Revolution, but they attest to the historical significance and symbolic connotation that Córdoba elicited in the state (Juárez Rivera 1987). This is the only explanation that makes sense, since the city was still underdeveloped, did not have the facilities to accommodate the three branches of government, and there were several, more adequate cities.

Until after the turn of the twentieth century, the economy of Córdoba depended primarily on the agriculture of the region. Sugarcane and coffee continued to be the main commercial crops, but rice and soybeans were also important. In addition, the region commercially produced mangoes, avocados, and several varieties of citrus, and cattle ranching complemented this diversified agricultural complex. As a market town,

Córdoba was a trading center that boasted many large stores and facilities catering to the needs of the region. This commercial component of the city remains but is much more diversified today. Both local entrepreneurs and foreign and Mexican businessmen who were attracted to Córdoba primarily from Mexico City, Puebla, and Monterrey fueled this economic growth. This confluence of factors has recently created an unprecedented degree of wealth for such a relatively small city (see Chapter 3).

DEMOGRAPHIC VARIABLES AND GEOGRAPHIC CONSIDERATIONS

The Córdoba region includes twenty-seven municipios of various sizes and populations. Five municipios still have Nahuatl-speaking Indian-traditional and Indian-transitional communities: Coscomatepec, Ixhuatlan del Café, and Chocamán on the lower slopes of Citlalteptl and Tequila and Zongolican to the south. There are no Totonac-speaking communities in the municipios of the coastal plains east of Córdoba; the last ones disappeared more than two generations ago. Until forty years ago, however, particularly in the municipio of Amatlán de los Reyes on the outskirts of Córdoba, there were Nahuatl-speaking peoples.

The ethnically Indian population comprises less than 8 percent of the total population of the region and is concentrated mostly in nucleated villages, without a local Mestizo population. There are a few mixed communities, but they are mostly municipal head towns; this is the case of Ixhuatlan del Café and Tequila. The latter communities, for example, are entirely Indian, whereas the head town has a large proportion of Mestizos. The same situation obtains in Zongolican and Coscomatepec. With the exception of Tequila, where all Indian communities are dispersed, most Indians in the region live in nucleated villages. In terms of secularization, about 30 percent are traditional Nahuatl-speaking communities, and the rest are communities in various degrees of transition.

The population in rural and urban environments is composed of various degrees of Mestizo phenotypes that range from the Indian standard of the region to the light, Caucasoid phenotype, popularly referred to as *criollos* (in this region and many others of central Mexico). Negroid features, particularly darker skin (as compared, say, with the Mestizo population of the Tlaxcala-Pueblan Valley), are quite noticeable, but there is also a gradation of phenotypes from unmistakably Negroid to light mulatto, difficult to pinpoint due to the Indian admixture. This generalization applies to urban centers and rural Mestizo communities, as the population of Indian villages does not exhibit any Negroid admixture. I cannot entirely explain this situation, but a likely hypothesis is that black slaves settled exclusively in the *tierra caliente* (hot lands, below 600 meters elevation), where they mixed with Indian and Mestizo populations, whereas the Indian communities that have survived to the present are all located in the tierra templada (between 700 and 1,600 meters) and the *tierra fria* (cold lands, between 1,600 and 2,700 meters). Except for criollos, many of whom are almost indistinguishable from Caucasoids, urban and rural Mestizo and Indian populations are phenotypically quite similar. This is the result of the urbanization that took place, particularly in Córdoba, during the second half of the twentieth century. This, of course, is much the same in all regions of the country with traditionally large Indian populations, for example, Chiapas, Oaxaca, and even Mexico City, which attracts Indian-traditional and Indian-transitional populations from all over the country.[1]

Notice that I have used the term "Caucasoid" to denote "white" populations. This term is not generally used to denote all people who are not Indian or black or all phenotypic admixtures of these racial categories. Rather, whites are referred to according to their national origins: Spaniards, Italians, Germans, French, Lebanese, Syrians, Palestinians—which accounts for most of the white peoples in the region. The term "white" is always used as an adjective (*una persona blanca,* a white person), never as a noun to refer to a phenotype. This is also a trait peculiar to many other regions of Mexico, although in Mexico City educated people occasionally use "white" to denote Caucasoid phenotypes.

People of European and Near Eastern extraction seldom retain their original national identity after the fourth generation in the country; at that point, individuals begin to refer to themselves as Mexican. It should be noted that Near Easterners are almost invariably phenotypically European, and it would be difficult to distinguish them from, say, Spaniards and other southern European-Mediterranean phenotypes, which exclude the Italians of the region, who are blondish, Germanic-looking phenotypes. As in all regions of Mexico, Near Easterners are generically referred to as Turcos, an artifact from the Ottoman Empire, from which the earliest immigrants arrived in Mexico. The total phenotypically white population of the region is difficult to determine, and my educated guess is that it comprises 10 percent of the total population. They are concentrated mostly in Córdoba and Fortin de las Flores, and a few are enfranchised in the other four cities or live in the country. Though there is no individual white ethnic identity, collective national identity is manifested by the persistence of free association groups, especially social clubs, of people of European and Near Eastern origin.

Beyond the Indians in their exclusive or mixed communities, there are no clear, well-bounded ethnic groups in the urban and rural sectors of the region. Thus ethnicity plays a rather limited role in the configuration of regional social stratification, with the exception that national origin plays a significant role in structuring the superordinate class of the region (see Chapter 3). In other words, with the exception of the two small sectors at the bottom and the top of the stratification system, the dynamics of class and race determine the regional organization of society.

The region for which Córdoba serves as a market city has a varied geographic and ecological setting. It extends from an altitude of 2,700 meters on the slopes of Mount Orizaba to 400 meters on the coastal plain; it encompasses cold lands, temperate lands, and hot lands. The largest part of the area comprises temperate lands, where coffee and sugarcane are cultivated, although the latter is also cultivated in the hot lands. The city of Córdoba is located on a hilly slope that extends from 600 to 850 meters in altitude. The other cities of the region are located at the following altitudes: Zongolica, 1,800 meters; Coscomatepec, 1,400 meters; Fortin de las Flores, 1,000 meters; Yanga, 500 meters; and Cuitlahuac, 400 meters. Most rural communities are located in the hot lands; a few, the poorest, in the cold lands above 1,600 meters. Because most of the commercial crops are cultivated there, the communities in the temperate lands are the most affluent. The best quality of coffee grows at an altitude of from 800 to 1,200 meters, and the highest yields of sugarcane are produced between 600 and 800 meters, that is, where the hot lands end and the temperate lands begin. Essentially the same obtains for the main commercial fruits: avocados, mangoes, pineapple, and papaya. Rice and bananas grow best in the hot lands but are not of great importance to the economy of rural communities. Staple crops (corn, beans, tomatoes, chili peppers, chayotes, etc.) are grown in both temperate and hot lands in moderate quantities, as peasants and farmers consider it more profitable to cultivate commercial crops and fruits. High-quality tobacco and soybeans are of moderate importance to the economy of the region. There are two large rice processing plants in Córdoba, but the grain comes from the neighboring hot lands toward the coast and to the south. Cattle ranching is moderately important, particularly in the hot lands, as are poultry farms in the temperate and cold lands.

Despite the growth of commerce and industry, the economy of Córdoba depends largely on agriculture. To some extent this is also true of the five small urban centers, three of which are noted for some local economic activity: floriculture in Fortin de las Flores, the manufacture of leather goods in Coscomatepec, and the manufacture of cigars in Yanga. The bulk of Córdoba's commerce is geared to the needs of the agricultural sector: small factories that produce agricultural implements, fertilizer plants, agricultural machinery agencies, automotive (truck) agencies, hardware stores, repair shops, and many specialized stores depend almost exclusively on the patronage of farmers and peasants.

Because for more than a generation foreign entrepreneurs and businessmen have been attracted to Córdoba by its diversified economy, the plutocratic wealth of the city is much greater than that of many cities of comparative size in central Mexico. The geographic location of Córdoba has also contributed to the growth of the transportation industry, which has been another important source of wealth. Since colonial times, Orizaba had been the most important city and commercial and industrial center in west-central Veracruz. This began to change in the middle of the twentieth century, and today Córdoba's more diversified economy has been the reason it has replaced Orizaba as the leading city in this part of Veracruz. Orizaba still has significant industries (breweries, a large paper-making factory, and several chemical and electronics factories), but all are owned by national and international companies.

I have touched only very briefly on the subsistence economy of the Indian and rural Mestizo communities and the ecological considerations it entails. I return to these matters in Chapter 5.

Chapter 3 | THE SUPERORDINATE SECTOR

The Ruling, Political, and Social Classes

The superordinate sector of society is composed of three subclasses: a small group of rich and powerful industrialists and businessmen engaged in manufacturing, trading, transportation, and agribusiness; an equally small group of local and state politicians; and an upper middle class of owners of large stores and small factories, small business concerns, and ranchers. These three groups constitute the local elite, in the social and economic sense, and together are a distinct segment of Córdoba and the region, although they do not necessarily constitute an integrated social class. It is thus best to describe them separately and as we proceed to analyze their social, economic, and other forms of interaction.

THE RICH AND POWERFUL: ORIGINS, SOURCES OF WEALTH, INFLUENCE, AND CONTROL

In the early 1940s Córdoba was a small, sleepy city with a small industrial establishment and a growing commercial base catering to the region. The hacienda system had been dismantled, and less than seven years after the initiation of the massive land reform, the economic influence of the hacendados had been drastically reduced. Unlike the hacendados of other regions of Mexico, the owners of the six or seven largest landed estates did not keep a residence in Córdoba, were enfranchised permanently in Mexico City, but once or twice a year resided in their hacienda mansions for a month or two at a time. Despite their absentee status, the hacendados and their families had a significant degree of social and economic control in the city and the region. Their economic control was derived not so much from patronizing the city's commercial ventures but from the regional economic power and political influence they had wielded for generations. On the other hand, their high status was the magnet that drew together the social life of the city, as the traditional, old established families of Córdoba, some of them tracing descent to the colonial period, gravitated to hacendado families when they were in town, assiduously attended celebrations on their landed estates, and were an integral part of the civic celebrations they sponsored in the city throughout the year. By the mid-1940s all of this had come to an end, and the departure of the hacendado families left a vacuum that had to be filled. This is the environment in which a new local and regional plutocracy arose.

To be sure, there had been a few rich, traditional upper-middle-class families in the city and countryside before this development, but though their lineage was impeccable, their wealth and influence were modest. This began to change during the presidency of Miguel Alemán, a native of the state of Veracruz. Although the description of Alemán and his cabinet as "Ali Baba and the forty thieves" was apt, the Alemán administration initiated an important phase in the industrialization and economic development of the country. The state of Veracruz experienced unprecedented growth, and by the late 1950s, Córdoba had become a bustling hub of entrepreneurial activity. Several small factories were established, the rather dramatic demographic growth of the city led to a much greater volume of commerce, and trade with the countryside increased greatly as a result of agribusiness, the growing importance of sugar mills, and the modernization of farming.

By the early 1960s, the economic elite of Córdoba, though few, was already relatively wealthy. They were owners of several coffee and rice processing plants, two foundries, and three large retail-wholesale stores. Ten years later, several cement, metallurgical, and automotive parts factories had been established; two regional sugar mills had become large-scale operations; and two processing plants monopolized the coffee business of central Veracruz. Up to this point, the new rich (an appropriate description as their fortunes dated back to no more than a generation) held from $10 million to $20 million. By the early 1980s, other sources of wealth had appeared: transportation, real estate, and hotel and supermarket chains. This completes the manifold sources of wealth of Córdoba's new plutocracy.

Although there were some millionaires in the region as early as the late 1950s, the largest fortunes of individuals and families (ranging from two to five nuclear families lineally or collaterally related) enfranchised in

Córdoba and other locales in its orbit of economic influence, were made during the past fifteen to twenty years. By summer 2000, when I finished the data collection for this book, there were approximately twenty-three individuals and families having fortunes ranging from $80 million to $350 million and eleven with fortunes ranging from $20 million to $60 million. This small group constitutes the local ruling class, the movers and shakers of the regional economy. As a result of the increasing democratization of Mexican society, however, this local ruling class does not wield the power and influence that hacendado families did until the Cárdenas land reform (1934–1940).[1]

At present the new rich derive their income from the following economic activities: (1) *comerciantes* (merchants and traders): wholesalers and owners of chain stores, usually hardware stores, paint outlets, and textile firms; (2) *industriales* (industrialists): owners of medium to large factories that produce beer, soft drinks, and comestible oil, process food and textiles, or manufacture automotive parts, machinery, chemicals, and fertilizers; (3) *transportes* (transportation): bus companies in the city and region and truck companies (short-haul operations to neighboring states and long-haul operations throughout Mexico); (4) *ingenios* (sugar mills): owners of large sugar mills (producing from 100,000 to 800,000 tons of refined sugar a year), including the production of rum and other alcoholic beverages; (5) *propiedades y bienes raices* (urban real estate in Córdoba and regional cities): owners and operators of office buildings, commercial buildings, tract housing, and up-scale urban developments; (6) *agricultores* (owners of large-scale farming and agribusiness): coffee, rice, wheat, fruits (mostly mangoes, bananas, and pineapple), sugarcane for the mills, and cattle ranching; (7) *hoteleros* (owners of individual and chains of hotels and restaurants) at the local, regional, state, and national levels; and (8) *negocios miscelaneos* (miscellaneous business): owners and operators of automotive dealerships, poultry farms, agricultural *maquila* (toll fee), and distributorships of beer, soft drinks, animal feeds, chemicals, and fertilizers, among others products.

The richest of the thirty-four individuals and families have a combined economic strategy that includes several of the foregoing enterprises, most often large-scale retailing (chains of hotels and supermarkets), industry, and real estate. On the other hand, almost invariably these millionaires pursue economic strategies that usually include combinations of two or three of the specific sources of wealth mentioned above. Significantly, the only major source of wealth that plutocrats have not been involved in is banking, as there are no regional banks and all business is conducted through the national banks operating out of Mexico City. Moreover, this plutocratic wealth was entirely locally generated, though probably most millionaires were not natives of the region, and several were not Mexican nationals. This composition of the local plutocracy is the rule rather than the exception in comparable regions of central Mexico with which I am acquainted.

This brings us to the social and ethnic extraction of the architects of the Córdoba regional plutocracy and how their wealth was amassed. In origin, development, and general configuration, provincial plutocracies are not different from the national plutocracy enfranchised in Mexico City; the main differences are the much greater degree of wealth and the more complex demographic and social setting in which the latter is embedded and the absence of plutocrats of political extraction and the fact that there was no local aristocratic model to emulate. These factors, as we shall see, translate, among other things, into a significantly different expressive culture.

The national plutocracy in the megalopolis of Mexico City was difficult to identify. Not so in Córdoba. The thirty-four individuals and nonresidential extended families constituting the local plutocracy comprise approximately 70 nuclear families and about 350 men, women, and children.[2] This group is well known and highly visible and can easily be identified by well-informed townspeople, who may guess, seldom accurately, the wealth of individual and family fortunes. Members of the upper middle class are especially prone to greatly exaggerate the fortunes of the plutocracy, which serve as the model to emulate. Members of the middle and working class, who are aware of the various enterprises that the plutocracy owns, almost invariably attribute dishonest means to its acquisition but have a grudging admiration for what plutocrats have achieved, which they regard as totally beyond their aspirations.

Specifically, what are the social origins, ethnic composition, career development, and main structural attributes of this local plutocracy? First, although there were a few moderately rich individuals before the mid-1950s, members of traditional families with roots in the pre-Porfirian era, none of the twenty-three largest fortunes in the region today had its origins before 1960. Some of the rich families of pre-1960 origin made it into the second rank of the rich today, but none has a fortune of more than $40 million. In other words, most of the fortunes of the plutocracy were amassed during the past twenty years, a few of them as recently as ten years ago. The wealth of the plutocracy has remained constant since then; no new fortunes have been made during the past six or seven years.

Second, plutocratic fortunes of the first rank have basically two beginnings: individual or family owners of one or two large enterprises going as far back as the late 1960s, which acquired plutocratic dimensions (putatively more than $100 million) between the early 1980s and the mid-1990s; or individuals of foreign extraction or from other Mexican states whose fortunes were amassed from 1980 to 1995. The former group combined wholesale commerce and agriculture (mostly sugar and coffee) or had vast real estate properties or medium-size industrial concerns. About thirteen plutocratic fortunes today are in this category. The latter group owns the largest industrial plants, transportation companies, supermarket chains, and hotel-restaurant chains and have diversified into other businesses. These ten fortunes constitute the richest sector of the plutocracy.

Third, the regional plutocracy enfranchised in Córdoba is not part of the richest fortunes made in the state of Veracruz. Beginning at the time of the Alemán administration, their owners gravitated to Mexico City. The three richest plutocrats came to Córdoba from other cities of central Mexico (Puebla, Veracruz, Guanajuato) with considerable capital, which was wisely invested, making them first-rank plutocrats in a very short period of time.

Fourth, the ethnic affiliation of plutocrats in Córdoba is quite varied, but more are of foreign than national extraction. Of the 34 millionaire individuals and families, thirteen are Mexican and twenty-one are of foreign extraction (first or second generation in Mexico). The breakdown of foreign individual and family millionaires is as follows: twelve are Spaniards (nine from Galicia, two from Castile, and one from Asturias), four are Lebanese, three are Syrian, and two are Cuban. A few individuals of Italian extraction had amassed regional fortunes on the order of $30 million to $50 million by the late 1980s, but they are now residents of Mexico City. They are second-generation descendants of immigrants brought to Mexico from northern Italy by Porfirio Díaz, who provided them with good agricultural land near the city of Huatusco.[3]

Incidentally, it was not surprising, after my experience with the plutocracy of the city of Puebla, that the preponderance of millionaire plutocrats of foreign extraction elicited so much resentment among Córdoba's middle class, especially among small businessmen and entrepreneurs. The situation, however, is complicated: people resent the foreigners' achievement of what they aspire to but have been unable to accomplish themselves but at the same time admire the foreigners' hard work, dedication, and sense of purpose. Subliminally (I use this term collectively, as

I have observed this syndrome in varied stratification contexts in central Mexico), Mexicans recognize the work ethic and commitment of the many foreigners who have become rich and powerful and blame themselves for being improvident, for lacking a penchant for hard work, and for being too inclined to enjoy the good life. One of my informants, the owner of a small hardware store, expressed the syndrome well when he referred to Córdoba's millionaires of Spanish extraction: "Llegan a México en alpargatas, con una mano por delante y otra por detras. Trabajan como burros, ahorran todo, no gastan en nada, y no se divierten. Rápido hacen dinero, y no es de sorprenderse que al poco tiempo se vuelven ricos. Mientras que nosotros los mexicanos somos flojos, no tenemos constancia, y somos demasiado dados a pasarla bien. Hacemos un poco de dinero, y en vez de ahorrar, no hallamos la hora en gastarnoslo todo." (They arrive in Mexico wearing hemp sandals, with no money and nothing to show. They work like donkeys, save every penny, do not spend money on anything, and do not have a good time. They quickly make money, and it is not surprising that in a short time they become rich. Whereas we Mexicans are lazy, have no perseverance, and are too inclined to have a good time. We make a little money, and instead of saving, we cannot wait to spend it all.) This may or may not be true of Spaniards and other foreigners, but it says a good deal about what many of the Mexican people think of themselves or, rather, how they rationalize the success of foreigners. I suspect that there is significant truth on both sides of the equation, and it would be worthwhile to investigate why foreigners, at the provincial but not so much at the national level, have been so successful as entrepreneurs. I have recorded many similar statements about foreign entrepreneurs, especially Spaniards, in many cities in central Mexico. The Spaniards, not surprisingly (given Mexicans' latent rancor about the colonial past), are the most severely resented, and the most common expression is that "vienen a México a hacer la America y a volver a explotarnos como lo hicieron por tres siglos" (they come to Mexico to enrich themselves and to exploit us again as they did for three centuries).

Fifth, I am not certain why there are no provincial plutocrats whose origins are in politics, whereas a significant number of national plutocrats made their fortunes while holding political office, particularly thirty or forty years ago. My guess is that the few local politicians, governors of states and cabinet ministers from the provinces, amassed their wealth while in residence in Mexico City and did not return to their natal states. Another consideration is that the opportunities for enrichment of local politicians enfranchised in the region are not enough to amass the immense fortunes associated with the national plutocracy (twenty-four billionaires among them). More significantly for the structural and expressive development of local plutocracies is the fact that by the time they began their ascent, fifty to sixty years ago, the aristocratic hacendados had emigrated to Mexico City and were no longer a local presence. As discussed below, local plutocracies, lacking an in situ model, have improvised on their own (in addition to emulating foreign plutocrats), mostly through business contacts and traveling abroad. This has resulted in "provincial" forms and patterns of behavior when compared to those of the sophisticated national plutocracy.

Sixth, it is important to consider the original class position of Córdoba plutocrats and when they began to amass their fortunes. The rags-to-riches scenario accounts for seven of the thirty-four plutocratic individuals; these are individuals of modest origins (probably working class to lower middle class) with little or no formal education and invariably of regional and state provenance. Among these seven are four Mexicans and three foreigners, all of them from central Veracruz. Except for one individual in this category, who is probably the richest man in the region, they are plutocrats of the second rank—individuals who, by dint of perseverance and imagination, amassed fortunes of up to $50 million in less than a generation.

The second group consists of individuals and families of middle-class origin, several educated at the elite universities of Mexico City, the Universidad Nacional Autónoma de México, the Universidad Iberoamericana, and the Instituto Politécnico de Monterrey. This group constitutes about two-thirds (twenty-two) of the plutocracy, and they are all plutocrats of the first rank. Ethnically, the group includes Mexicans and foreigners of all the nationalities mentioned above. Two plutocrats have no formal education, but they are a distinct exception, as this group as a whole is the best formally educated, and this is particularly the case with plutocratic families who have sent their children to study abroad, either in the United States or in England. This nucleus of young, recently married plutocrats, ranging in age from twenty-five to thirty-five, are regarded, by their own subclass and by the well informed in Córdoba, as the most professional and innovative and worthy of emulation.

The third group, five families in all, includes individual members with the best class position at the beginning of their plutocratic careers. Except for a second-generation Spanish family, the other four were Mexican. Two of the latter date from the Porfiriato, and the other two trace their descent to the colonial period and have been prominent in Córdoba since. These families constitute a small nucleus of about eighteen collaterally and lineally related nuclear families and are universally regarded as "familias antiguas y de linaje" (old and distinguished families), the closest to a socially exalted elite in regional society. Although they are not necessarily prominent, as they are economically plutocrats of secondary rank, they are much sought after socially by the richest plutocrats.

Seventh, the regional plutocracy resides in Córdoba and the nearby community of Fortin de las Flores. The plutocracy is clustered primarily in the four upscale sections of Córdoba: Club de Golf, La Alameda, San José, and Nueva Córdoba. Fortin, five miles from Córdoba and 250 meters higher, has always been a residential city because of the lushness of the surrounding landscape and mild climate. This residential pattern is shared, of course, by the three sectors of the regional elite and the most affluent people of the middle class. As discussed in Chapter 1, residence in the Mexican stratification system is not as exclusive and significant an index of class membership as it is in the United States, and a considerable number of elite residences are located in average sections of the city. A few members of the Córdoba elite have country homes, but this is not nearly as widespread a practice as among the national plutocracy, for whom it is de rigueur to have a country retreat. On the other hand, most plutocrats have bought houses in the border areas of California, Arizona, and Texas, where they reside for a month or more every year.

Some of the richest plutocrats have residences that may qualify as mansions — one or two city blocks of beautifully landscaped grounds in the midst of which is located a one- or two-story house with twenty to thirty rooms. However, the average plutocratic house is more modest and not nearly as ostentatious. In fact, the houses of politicians and those of the more affluent upper-middle-class families are quite similar. The residences of all three sectors of the regional elite are architectural disasters: pretentious copies of styles totally inadequate to the region's tropical or semitropical climate. This is the norm rather than the exception for the contemporary provincial architecture of Mexico outside the capital, despite the fact that Mexico boasts world-class architects. The decoration and display of regional elite houses is not much better, and it is more appropriate to discuss it in the section on expressive analysis.

Eighth, the wealth of the plutocracy has translated into differential power and control in the economic, political, and social affairs of Córdoba and the region. As I stated above, the new plutocracy that emerged after the 1934–1940 land reform has not had the same influence as the old hacendado class had for nearly a generation after the onset of the Mexican

Revolution, despite the great changes that had taken place. Beyond this assertion, I can only give partial answers to the question of the plutocracy's influence.

Socially, the plutocracy as a whole maintains a rather low profile, both individually and collectively. There are no clubs that plutocrats exclusively patronize, and the four or five clubs in the city, primarily the Golf Club and two social clubs founded by upper-middle-class families of Spanish descent, are open to the local elite as a whole. The household, rather, is the hub of their social life, and celebrations almost invariably take place there. These are elaborate affairs, to which politicians and upper-middle-class people are invited; the latter, especially, constitutes the social support group of plutocratic families. This is the role in which the upper middle class has been cast vis-à-vis the rich and powerful (be it an aristocracy, a plutocracy, or any other superordinate group) everywhere in the context of Western society and its extensions.[4] Again, these are aspects of the social life of the plutocracy best discussed in the expressive analysis section. On the other hand, the social saliency that the hacendados had in the city is a thing of the past, as plutocrats invariably try to maintain a low public presence. The only public involvement of individual plutocrats is in occasional acts of philanthropy on behalf of institutions or "cultural" and educational activities.

Politically, the influence of the plutocracy is considerably greater, which, together with their control of the regional economy, justifies the appellation "local ruling class." Since its inception more than two generations ago, no member of the plutocracy has held political office, and a certain inherent antipathy characterizes the conception plutocrats as a whole have of politicians. Nevertheless, plutocrats cultivate office holders as a strategy to safeguard or advance their economic interests, mostly involving the relaxation of city or state regulations and securing choice locations for their businesses, factories, and other enterprises. Their relationship may be characterized as polite, almost sub rosa, but plutocrats would not hesitate to coerce politicians when necessary, sweetening this coercion, of course, with the traditional *mordida* (bribe). Social contact with politicians is limited and almost invariably takes place in the home.

The wealth of the plutocracy is present everywhere, as they are the only large employers in the region and control the manufacture of the most important commodities, the distribution of the major items of consumption, the transportation network, and the regional agriculture. The concentration of wealth in the Córdoba regional plutocracy is comparatively greater than in Mexico City, and, based on my knowledge of the Puebla and Jalapa regions, it is quite likely that the same obtains in many regions of the country with a similar manufacturing-agricultural base. In keeping with their concern for maintaining a low profile, the economic power and influence plutocrats wield is exercised discretely, even the limited philanthropy in which they engage. Unlike the much more diversified and sophisticated ambience of Mexico City, in which the plutocracy engages in the public exhibition and display characteristically associated with the rich and powerful, the Córdoba regional plutocracy is well aware that such a strategy would not be to its economic advantage, hence, as one informant put it, the concern with "pasar desapercibidos" (maintaining a low profile).

Finally, small as it is, the Córdoba regional plutocracy is not in any sense an integrated group and does not exhibit a consciousness of its own class. This lack of cohesion and self-identity may be explained by the following main factors: the diversity of original class position, the educational differences that go with it, and the ethnic diversity of the group. There is a degree of consciousness of kind in being rich and having influence, but it does not result in collective, concerted action. There is, however, a distinct sense of elite self-identification that the plutocracy shares with the other two superordinate sectors of regional society (see below).

Here I have described what is most distinctive and structurally exclusive of the plutocratic sector. There are other aspects that the plutocracy shares with the political sector and the upper middle class, and they are discussed below. The expressive analysis concludes the description of the three sectors of the regional superordinate class.

THE POLITICIANS: SOCIAL ORIGINS, CAREER DEVELOPMENT, AND DEGREE OF CONTROL

The political sector is small, the most transitory, and hence the most difficult to isolate. I have stated that plutocrats do not vie for political office; conversely, "professional" politicians, that is, individuals who have held several offices above a certain level, do not become plutocrats; or, as I explained it, at the provincial level the opportunities to amass wealth while in office are limited (to put it crudely, there are fewer opportunities for graft as compared with the national context). Almost invariably, however, regional politicians are reasonably enriched through graft and bribery while holding political office. The noxious attitude that holds an honest politician in disdain is changing, part of a new concept of citizenship that is beginning to assert itself. (See chapters 4 and 5.)

Who are the local politicians, and how can they be conceived as a distinct group affecting Córdoba and the region? At the top are the four congressmen (*diputados federales*) and the nine state representatives (*diputados estatales*) of the districts comprising the region. Just below these are the local delegate of the federal attorney general's office (Procurador General de la República) and local delegates of several ministries (Hacienda [Internal Revenue Service], Industria y Comercio [Industry and Commerce], Communicaciones y Transporte [Transportation], Agricultura y Recursos Humanos [Agriculture and Human Resources], etc.). Next are the mayor of Córdoba and the seven members of the city council; after them, the mayors of Coscomatepec, Yanga, and Cuitlahuac, the three largest cities after Córdoba. Unofficially, there are other regional politicians, a former state governor and two or three former federal senators who reside in Córdoba and its environs and exert significant influence.

Local and state officials, on the one hand, and federal officials, on the other, exert different degrees of leverage and control and are differentially important to plutocrats and are related to them in distinct areas of action. They must therefore be treated separately in order to determine the nature of the interaction between these two sectors of the regional superordinate class.

Let us take local and state officials first. Estate representatives, the mayor of Córdoba, its seven councilmen, and the mayors of the three main regional cities are all locally enfranchised and control the everyday political and economic life of the region: the passage of local legislation concerning taxation, urban development, zoning, public works, commerce, primary and secondary local and state education, traffic, local police and surveillance, standards of public behavior, public health, and several other functions of city and regional government. Although there is a degree of state and federal control, it is mostly in the hands of the local authorities to set up the necessary mechanisms to enforce legislation, which includes a local police force, a court system, and a diversified bureaucracy. Thus the political power of local and state officials is of primary importance to plutocrats, who wish to influence legislation and enforcement so as to enhance and protect their economic interests. The wealth they control, and the power derived from it, makes the Córdoba plutocracy a local ruling class without having to exercise the political functions of government. In other words, plutocrats are able to generate the most propitious conditions for their business enterprises. With the connivance of local officials, plutocrats bend the rules (e.g., rerouting the construction of a road to connect a factory to a highway), quite frequently bypassing them altogether (e.g., disregarding zoning regulations for many kinds of economic enterprises), and occasionally having a voice in the passage of new legislation when the situation requires it (e.g., modifying local taxation and commerce statutes). This, of course, is done by means of bribery and other forms of graft that, in time-honored fashion, very few officials are able to resist. It is difficult to say whether plutocrats offer bribes to officials or whether the latter in subtle ways let the former know that an outcome requires an appropriate bribe. The game of graft is so well tuned and institutionalized that it is irrelevant to ask who initiates it. As a result, officials may not become millionaires, as happens at the national level, but when they leave office they are quite wealthy by local standards.

Federal officials, the four congressmen, the local attorney general, and the delegates of the various ministries are not enfranchised in Córdoba and usually leave the region after their terms in office. They do not control local politics and have little influence in the conduct of regional business but are nonetheless of great importance to the economic interests of plutocrats, since many of their largest enterprises transcend the region and are regulated by federal agencies. Federal officials are therefore important to plutocrats, who cultivate them while they are in office, but their relationship with them is different from that with local and state officials. As they do not have any roots in the region and have no local vested interest to safeguard, plutocrats have no need to establish social relationships with them. Plutocrats relate to them strictly as public officials who can be bribed in the course of doing business. The nature of the graft involved is the same as that with local and state officials; the bribes are probably larger, but they are not as frequent. In smoothing the conduct of state and national business, the most important officials to cultivate are the delegate of the attorney general office and the delegates of the Hacienda and Industria y Comercio ministries. These are the federal agencies most directly connected with the wide-ranging enterprises of Córdoba plutocrats, or in whose purview it is to regulate interstate commerce and settle labor disputes.

Of course, office holders have constituencies to whom they are related in a variety of ways and who are totally unrelated to the other two sectors of the region's superordinately placed, the plutocracy and upper middle class. For the working class and the dispossessed, politicians serve as sources of patronage, and to a significant extent, they are still admired and regarded as symbols of upward mobility despite the aura of corruption that they project. Patronage does not represent a source of wealth for politicians; rather, the bribery that patronage entails is associated with the bureaucrats people have to negotiate with in order to get access to politicians. By contrast, most members of the middle class, as it is defined below, have contempt for politicians as being ineffectual and corrupt and avoid official contact with them whenever possible. It should be emphasized at this point that bribery and graft are the daily bread of the citizenry in dealing with the bureaucracy, the police, and all local, state, and federal government offices in order to expedite matters or to avoid penalties and fines.

The class position of elected officials exhibits significant variation. Until about 1950 or so, politicians almost invariably came from the middle or upper middle class. It was not until about 1970 that significant numbers of individuals from the working class became engaged in politics. At present, about 40 percent of elected officials come from the working class; their parents, usually at great economic sacrifice, have subsidized their higher education, either in universities in the state of Veracruz or in the elite universities of Mexico City. Also, the path of the humble individuals who by dint of economic acumen become successful businessmen on a small or medium scale is another means to involvement in politics. Politicians whose origins are in the working class are most commonly found in the cities and towns of the region, whereas the politicians enfranchised in Córdoba are almost exclusively of middle- and upper-middle-class origin and monopolize not only the city council but also the regional offices; essentially, they are state representatives. What these two categories of politicians share are the same career paths: a university education, usually in law, medicine, or engineering, or a modicum of success in a business enterprise. Regardless of class origin, politicians — and politics in general — are regarded as corrupt, self-serving, and ineffectual by most of the middle and upper middle class, whereas they are still a source of identification and inspiration for the working class and the dispossessed.

What is the control exercised by the political sector, independent of the influence of plutocrats (irrespective of the lack of respect bordering on antagonism of the well-off middle and upper middle classes), and what influence do they have on the body politic? These also are difficult questions, and my answers must be tentative. They are undoubtedly in control of the finances of the cities, towns, and municipios of the region; and they largely decide what public projects to undertake and have the strongest voice in changing or introducing new statutes. In the exercise of these governing activities, elected officials vary greatly in degree of control. At the "folk" level, that is, in the rural municipios, elected officials have little or no control, as there are few if any locally generated revenues; the public works, schools, health, and other facilities are provided by the state and/or federal government. Concomitantly, there is insignificant or no graft. In the towns and small cities of the region, the degree of control is higher, given the larger size and heterogeneity of the population, in which kinship, compadrazgo, and other folk institutions are institutionally insufficient. Locally generated revenues are considerable, and corruption exists. In Córdoba, the economic and bureaucratic center of the region, elected officials have the greatest control, as the residual effect of folk institutions becomes negligible. Graft becomes widespread, as revenue is greater than the combined revenues of all municipios, towns, and cities in the region.

On the other hand, the political sector of elected and influential former office holders does not by itself formulate governing policy affecting the economic, social, educational, health, and "cultural" life of the region. To a large extent, policy is dictated by the state of Veracruz, and in this process the local plutocracy, with extensive state connections, has a strong voice. Beyond the environment of graft and corruption that binds the political class and the plutocracy, the domain of policy is diagnostic in characterizing the relationship of these two classes of the superordinate sector of the region: the former exercises limited control; the latter is the most powerful interest group and shapes the public affairs of the region. From this standpoint, the plutocracy is a ruling class by any definition of the term.

It was extremely difficult to adequately assess what I have called the political class of Córdoba and the region as a group exhibiting a degree of interdependence or at least a sense of organic cohesion. First, I should make explicit that by "political class," I am referring to those in office in any current administration and past office holders who have managed to retain a measure of political influence. At the municipal level this does not obtain, and whether there is such an entity as a political class is highly unlikely; if it does exist, it is strictly a local phenomenon.[5] Thus the regional political class is composed of the estate senators and the mayors and city councils of Córdoba, Yanga, Cuitlahuac, Fortin, and two other towns. This group is small, and in any administration there are probably no more than fifty individuals in office and twenty-five or thirty past officials—until five or six years ago dominated by the PRI but now including the more influential members of the PAN and PRD. When the PRI monopolized the region's political offices, the group was more unified, and one could properly call it an effective political class. During the past decade, the situation has become amorphous, and whatever concerted effort at political action was possible when the PRI was in control has vanished, and it is doubtful that it will ever be the same again. What will probably not change, despite the avowed protestations of the PAN and the PRD that they will not follow the PRI's pattern of corruption, is the bond with the plutocracy, traditionally characterized by bribery and graft. Be this as it may, at present or in the near future it is unlikely that the political class in Córdoba will acquire a significant collective structure that would independently affect government policy and exercise power and influence solely for the benefit of the regional constituency.

THE UPPER MIDDLE CLASS: SOCIAL AND ECONOMIC COMPOSITION AND SIGNIFICANCE

Even in modern industrial countries, the upper middle class, mostly defined as an economic entity (as is the case in the United States but less so in Europe and perhaps in other industrialized countries of the world, where it retains a significant social-expressive component), is always very small, probably never exceeding more than 5 to 7 percent of the total population. In the Córdoba region, it is even smaller. Let us first determine the demographic composition of the local upper middle class and then the economic and social attributes that define it.

My rough estimate is that the upper middle class of Córdoba and the region is about 1.5 percent of the total population of about 800,000, that is, no more than 12,000 people, or roughly 2,500 nuclear families. The overwhelming majority of them are enfranchised in Córdoba and Fortin, but a few reside in the other cities of the region and in the countryside. The great majority of upper-middle-class families achieved this socioeconomic status within the past forty years, but it was not possible to determine what their annual disposable income was when this happened, as I have determined for the ethnographic present. It is clear, however, that the demographic growth of the upper middle class took place during the past twenty-five years, during which it grew by more than 50 percent.

What does it mean to define a class based on economic or social-expressive terms or a combination of both? As I stated in Chapter 2, approaching the study of class on the basis of purely structural factors results in an incomplete account of stratification. To put it differently, specifying the upper middle class of Córdoba as a segment of the population exclusively based on wealth, education, occupation, and other so-called objective attributes would leave out an important diagnostic aspect, both as an account of the class itself and for conceptualizing its relationship to other classes of the stratification system. To complement this operation, a social-expressive component must be generated that specifies so-called subjective factors. Once this is achieved, we have a more complete description of a social class endogenously and exogenously: its internal configuration is established with respect to visibility, class consciousness, and collective self-perception; its external configuration is situated as an object of emulation and/or to cultivate socially by other social classes. Let us specify what this signifies for the Córdoba upper middle class. The structural composition of the upper middle class is as follows.

Economically, it includes people (specifically, nuclear families) with annual disposable incomes of $100,000 to $200,000, derived from a variety of sources: large retail stores, small factories, health clinics (*santorios*), car and truck dealerships, farm equipment dealerships, real estate, medium-size farming (coffee, rice, avocados, mangoes, citrus, etc.) and ranching, and a few other operations. In addition, a few of the top practicing professionals in the region, primarily lawyers, physicians, accountants, and engineers, who may also own businesses associated with their professions such as notary public offices (*notarías*, a crucial aspect of Mexican bureaucratic life), accounting firms, and consulting firms, belong to this category.

With the exception of the professionals, who represent less than 8 percent, the upper middle class is not the best trained group in the region, but they are the best "educated" (*instruidos, cultos*). What does this mean? On the one hand, the upper middle class and the plutocracy are as a whole not the best trained sectors of the population; that is, as a rule they do not have professional degrees. This has been changing during the past generation, however, as most men and women under thirty have attended local universities or elite universities in Mexico City, and considerable numbers have been trained in the United States and England. On the other hand, these two sectors of the superordinate class are unquestionably the best educated, that is, the best read and the best informed, and they generally have a passable grasp of history, literature, philosophy, and the arts. This is precisely what the terms *instruido* and *culto* denote in Mexican Spanish everywhere.[6] Education, so conceived, is acquired at home, part of the family tradition, as attested by the extensive libraries in many plutocratic and upper-middle-class households. Or it may be the product of the extensive travels abroad that characterize the leisure life of these two groups, especially plutocrats.

Residentially, there is nothing exclusive about the upper-middle class that I have not already discussed about the plutocracy; that is, they reside in the most upscale sections of Córdoba and Fortin, the architecture is not attuned to the tropical and semitropical environment of the region, and residences are pretentious and kitschy (*cursi*). There are a few exceptions to this generalization: a few traditional upper-middle-class families still reside in elegant *casas porfirianas* (houses built between 1880 and 1910 during the dictatorship of Porfirio Díaz) near the civic center of Córdoba. Incidentally, these are the only examples of outstanding domestic architecture in the area; unfortunately, no more than a dozen or so have survived.

In terms of power and wealth, little can be said about the upper middle class. They are affluent by any standard, they are pillars of the immediate economic life of the city and region, but they are not a significant voice in influencing the life of the people at large, as are plutocrats and the political class; nor do they significantly control specific sectors of social and economic life. The upper middle class is the most apolitical sector of the stratification system; only a few have been elected to political office, and they are the most vocal critics of the political establishment. Their worldview is centered on making money and maintaining a high standard of living, but as they pursue these endeavors, like everybody else, they are drawn into the political and bureaucratic web of bribery and graft. Racially and phenotypically, together with the minuscule plutocracy, the upper middle class is the most homogeneous sector of the city and the region. This sector of the population is composed mostly of Caucasoid and light Mestizo phenotypes and only a few (about 5 percent of the total) are dark Mestizo and Indian phenotypes.[7] With the exception of the political class, which has a more mixed composition, this is the rule rather than the exception in the composition of comparable local, provincial ruling classes of central Mexico. I arrived at this conclusion based on my observations in the cities and surrounding regions of Puebla, Jalapa, Veracruz, Orizaba, Pachuca, and Atlixco, which was confirmed in my intensive study of the Mexican aristocracy and plutocracy enfranchised in Mexico City. I explain this by the general rule that the higher the social class, the more European phenotypes are likely to constitute its membership, which applies throughout the country. This is the result of the colonial mentality that has permanently burdened a fundamentally Mestizo-Indian society with standards of appearance, beauty, and behavior that are not its own. The corollary is that the more European an individual looks, the more likely he or she is to rise on the social scale and the greater the probability of success in entrepreneurial and professional activities. It is no wonder, then, that the Mexican stratification system, from top to bottom, is rampant with the manipulation of phenotypes to enhance opportunities of all kinds and in the perennial game of upward mobility.

The plutocracy and the upper middle class are very conscious of their mostly European extraction and consider themselves white collectively; this, of course, includes the relatively small group of plutocrats and upper-middle-class individuals of Near Eastern extraction. In the typical fashion described in Chapter 1, the whitening syndrome obtains and serves as a mechanism to minimize the somatic traits exhibited by the few Mestizo and Indian phenotypes. Collectively, this small sector of the population is unquestionably racist, but this racism is tempered by the fact that it is rarely acted on. Privately, however, many maintain that their economic success is attributed to being white and that, by contrast, the laziness, improvidence, and lack of perseverance of most Mexicans (usually indiscriminately lumping together Mestizo and Indian populations) are equally factors of race. I want to point out that this tempered racism is also exhibited by the few white middle-class individuals, who usually rationalize the fact that they are not wealthier and have better social position by pointing to the corrupting effect of politicians and other unrealistic constructions.

What are the main characteristics of the upper middle class by itself and in relation to the other two sectors of the superordinate class of Córdoba and the region? First, and briefly, a few remarks about its composition and ranking. At the top, there is a small group of traditional families, perhaps fifty, whose class standing dates from the Porfiriato, several of them extending their roots to colonial times; they are among the less economically affluent but the most prominent in the region, and all of them are enfranchised in Córdoba. They were the immediate social support group of hacendado families and today hold that position vis-à-vis the plutocracy. Next, probably 35 percent of all upper-middle-class families, whose standing is more recent, although some trace their roots to the turn of the twentieth century, fall in the middle range of economic affluence and have significant social prestige. They are enfranchised in Córdoba, and there are a few in all cities of the region; they constitute the social elite, but their significance does not transcend the local scene. The majority of families today are those with the lowest original class position. They invariably acquired upper-middle-class status during the past generation and, as such, rank the lowest on the social scale. These families are found in all the cities of the region, they are the most affluent, and, in Córdoba, they own the most important retail outlets and are the most noted professionals.

As a social entity, the upper middle class is the most visible sector of the regional stratification system; it is collectively the most identifiable group in the public life of the region, considering that the plutocracy, though well known, keeps a low profile. In other words, the upper middle class is what the middle class in Mexico City calls "la sociedad," that is, the socially prominent, those who are in the limelight and whose doings are reported in the newspapers. Patronizing fairs, attracting well-known bands to Córdoba, organizing art exhibits, and other such cultural events are mostly associated with upper-middle-class individuals who take a public interest in the city or take part in these activities as a way to promote their businesses. The two local dailies servicing the region report the social life of upper-middle-class families, who are perceived by the bulk of the population as the social and cultural leaders of the community.

Upper-middle-class families are the most apparent models of upward mobility for the middle and working classes. Their wealth and social standing are perceived as attainable goals for those who are willing to sacrifice and work hard (the exorbitant wealth, by local standards, of the plutocracy is considered an unattainable dream). The wealth and power of plutocrats and politicians is considered ill gained, whereas the affluence of the upper middle class is considered by the majority of the population as having been earned by honest means and hard work. Moreover, most people subliminally harbor an appreciation of good lineage and tradition, embodied in the old, traditional, upper-middle-class families. Thus middle- and working-class people look up to these families and still speak of them as socially exalted; upper-middle-class people regard them as the social leaders of the group; and the plutocracy cultivates them as a validating symbol of their recently acquired power and wealth. In Córdoba and the region, this small group of families that trace their standing to the Porfiriato is the closest to the concept of "social class" in Aron's (1966, 204) definition of the term.

Finally, what is culturally shared by the three classes of the superordinate sector? First, they are the most conservatively religious sector of the stratification system. With very few exceptions, they are orthodox Catholics; there are fewer than a dozen Muslim and Jewish families and no Protestants in the superordinate sector. By "orthodox," I mean that their Catholicism has few of the folk beliefs that characterize the religiosity of everyone else, but as a whole they are not necessarily assiduous churchgoers. On the contrary, a few of them, mostly politicians, are agnostic, and some are anticlerical, voicing that the church and priests are not doing a good job in counteracting the inroads of Protestant evangelism. This is a concern that I heard expressed in a variety of ways, particularly among the more pious families of the upper middle class. The most commonly verbalized objection is that the hierarchy is not aggressively counteracting conversion, implicitly asserting that, regardless of the freedom of religion that exists in Mexico today, evangelists have no right to proselytize in a traditionally Catholic country. Although as a rule they celebrate the manifold events of the religious annual and life cycles, they are not nearly as ritualistic as the middle and lower sectors of society.

Kinship and the organization of the household are essentially the same in the three classes of the superordinate sector. Kinship is reckoned bilaterally, and there are no operational units beyond the household, except for a loosely organized nonresidential extended family (Nutini 1968) that may include from five to as many as nine lineally and collaterally related households. The nonresidential extended family has mildly significant social functions, mainly as a support group in the celebration of events in the annual and life cycles, but it does not have the organic constitution that the unit has in the folk context. The patrilocal extended family household may occasionally be realized, but it is of short duration, seldom lasting more than two or three years, long enough for the young married couple to get on their feet economically. The nuclear family household is the norm, and it is always small: parents and seldom more than three unmarried children. The number of children per nuclear family today is small, the ideal being two or three, while two generations ago nuclear families were large, and six or seven offspring per family was not unusual. The number of children a family has is a purely pragmatic matter, and religious considerations are seldom if ever a significant factor in procreation. In summary, the superordinate sector of Córdoba and the region is, as a whole, culturally uniform, but there are behavioral differences among its component classes, as is apparent in the discussion that follows.

EXPRESSIVE ANALYSIS

The interrelationship of race, class, and ethnicity in Mexico is an encompassing generator of expression. How is this realized in the specific context of Córdoba's superordinate sector of society? And what are the manifestations of the whitening syndrome, the configuration of expressive emulation, and the organization of the expressive array in terms of the exclusive and inclusive domains? I shall analyze these domains separately and establish the consequences they entail.

Race

The plutocracy and the upper middle class perceive themselves as phenotypically white and quite often refer to themselves as European, even those who are of Near Eastern extraction.[8] This is essentially true, as very few exhibit Amerindian or Negroid traits, which is not the case with the political class, a mixed group that does exhibit these traits. Moreover, like politicians throughout Mexico, they cultivate the image of being of humble origins, and even if they are phenotypically white, they refer to themselves in public as Mestizo. Thus it is quite proper to regard the superordinate sector of Córdoba society as being of European extraction, given that the urban political class is so small.

Therefore, largely within the confines of a group uniformly perceived and self-perceived as phenotypically white, plutocrats and the upper middle class extend social recognition in terms of somatic appearance. In other words, with the exception of politicians, the main attribute that characterizes the superordinately placed is the kind of somatic uniformity that determines class consciousness and leads to the establishment of social ties and significant operational networks. More significant for understanding the mechanisms of superordinate class formation is that expressive manipulation takes place in this context, and individuals who exhibit somatic characteristics that deviate from the phenotypical standard of the group tend to be minimized, that is, are whitened and made more appealing. The whitening syndrome and allied forms of phenotypic-social manipulation are realized in manifold contexts and situations at all levels of the stratification system, as discussed later.

But how, specifically, is the whitening syndrome realized in the superordinate sector? First, the perceived composition of the political class ranges from Indian to European but is stereotyped as an essentially Mestizo sector beyond the *tolerable* phenotypical manipulation of "white" plutocrats and upper-middle-class people. This is the main reason why the political class of Córdoba is the least socially integrated. The superordinate sector as a whole, however, is perceived by the overwhelming majority of the population as the "whitest" sector of society, not only on justified somatic grounds but also by virtue of the power and wealth it denotes. This position in society, according to the ideology of race and ethnicity, commands, all things being equal, more honor and respect than are accorded to the common citizen. It should be noted, though, that the subservient attitude of the common citizen is changing rapidly, but it nonetheless attests to the persistence of ancien régime traits that in Europe and the United States have almost totally disappeared. In Mexico, it is still present in varying degrees, but it is most pronounced in rural and provincial environments.

Second, in the endogenous context of plutocratic/upper-middle-class social interaction, the whitening syndrome is of limited incidence, given the phenotypical uniformity of the group. It is occasionally realized, however, for two main reasons. First, it is used to incorporate politicians into the group when they exhibit "tolerable" deviations from the phenotypic standard. In the course of maximizing some entrepreneurial activity, close social interaction with them is deemed necessary, and it thus becomes important that a particular politician and his family be perceived as close phenotypically to the average members of the group. This is always manageable in that the majority of important politicians who are sought after are light Mestizo phenotypes, making the whitening perceptibly within the unspoken rules of manipulation, discussed below. It goes without saying that this is exclusively realized at the highest urban level; what happens at the folk level is discussed in Chapter 5. Second, whitening occurs when the offspring of plutocrats and upper-middle-class people marry those who are phenotypically Mestizo, as occasionally happens, and it is considered de rigueur to establish close kinship relations with in-laws. This primarily takes place when young men and women go away to college and interact with the entire phenotypical spectrum of Mexican society. It may also happen when marriage is contracted with an offspring of a Mestizo politician or of a well-to-do person of middle-class extraction. The whitening syndrome involving kinship considerations is always stronger and more permanent than that involving political considerations.

Third, the phenotypical manipulations that accompany the syndrome are culturally quite patterned; they involve self-directed and group-directed behavior and activities to induce people to regard an individual or family as European-looking. This is achieved by emphasizing cultural factors that either lead people to perceive actual somatic features differently or to overlook them altogether. A couple of examples will make this clear. One of the most common strategies is to emphasize the refinement of behavior, good breeding, and elegance of the individual to be whitened, ethnocentrically assuming that the whiter a person is, the more he or she is endowed with these qualities. The aim is to induce the people of one's social set to believe that the individual, despite phenotypical deviation, is worthy of being accepted. Since the superordinately placed share the syndrome, whitening an individual or family becomes an exercise of psychological euphemism. Another strategy is to enhance the racial background of the individual being whitened by asserting that for two or more generations his or her ancestors were of pure European stock but that there was some mixture before and that the phenotypical deviation exhibited by the individual is recessive, or as it is expressed in the vernacular, he or she is a *salto atras* (lit., "a backward jump," a reference to one of the categories of the eighteenth-century *casta* system). This is most successful when individuals are from another region, but there are variations of this strategy that make it more effective when individuals are locals. Be this as it may, sociophenotypical manipulation is always aimed at acceptance by the group and as a palliative for the individual or family being whitened.

Class

In Chapter 2 I discussed vicariousness as a fundamental aspect of social stratification and mobility whose most determinant manifestation is expressive emulation. In other words, expressive emulation underlies the realization of aspirations to upward mobility and to a significant extent shapes class consciousness. Although the entailments of expressive emulation are the same in any stratification system, their actualization and ramification vary as people move from one class to another. In the remainder of this section I analyze how expressive emulation is realized in the superordinate sector and the role it plays in achieving elite status. Three points are discussed: the sources of emulation, what they signify endogenously and exogenously, and a comparison of the expressive array of the Córdoba superordinately placed with that of the aristocracy-plutocracy/upper middle class of Mexico City. The aim of the latter point is to assess the differences and similarities of provincial and national expressive culture.

The hacendado class, which had a social presence in the Córdoba region until the early 1940s, was a rather limited source of emulation for the nascent local plutocracy. On the one hand, its lifestyle was impossible to replicate after the demise of the hacienda system; on the other, the local plutocracy was still too embryonic to have been directly influenced by the hacendado families. Rather, the influence was through the traditional upper middle class, which was closely associated with the haciendas, where the elite social life of the region was centered. For generations, traditional upper-middle-class families had served as the social support of hacendados, and in this ambience they emulated the aristocratic hacendados. By the early 1940s these families had a sophisticated expressive array that was derived largely from the hacendados. Its most salient domains extended from forms of entertainment, household decoration, and sports to presentation of the self, dress, and a large ensemble of patterns of behavior that ranged from elegant celebrations of the events of life and annual cycles to refined comportment on many social and religious occasions. This is the hacendado expressive complex that through the agency of the traditional upper middle class served as the local model for the developing plutocracy from then on. Two generations later, roughly after the early 1990s, the traditional upper middle class and the upper middle class that developed coterminously with the plutocracy were not affluent enough to realize several of these expressive domains, which together with expressive domains of other origins became the exclusive preserve of the plutocracy.

Another source of expressive emulation for the local plutocracy has been travel and business abroad, particularly during the past fifteen years, when the wealth of plutocrats, by local standards, reached enormous proportions. Plutocrats traveled to Europe and other parts of the world, but their business enterprises were almost exclusively in the border states of the United States. The expressive domains that plutocrats learned abroad, in direct contact with other plutocrats and indirectly through their travels, are essentially those that characterize plutocratic circles everywhere.

The closest analogy of a superordinate source of emulation in the United States for the plutocracy during the past two generations, that is, the equivalent of an American "aristocracy," are the Boston Brahmins, the Virginia gentry, and the old New York Dutch establishment. During the past generation, however, the rapidly generated immense wealth of the newest plutocracy has occasioned the creation of a new expressive culture. This is already afoot in the national plutocracy enfranchised in Mexico City, and the same, on a significantly reduced scale, in poor country cousin fashion, is happening in provincial Córdoba, exacerbated by relative isolation.

The original purveyors of expressive emulation (the dying aristocracy in Europe and Mexico City, the American "aristocracy," the traditional upper middle class in Córdoba and in many Mexican provincial environments) have been eliminated from this expressive game, as I have ascertained for the superordinate sectors of Mexico City and Córdoba society. They simply do not have the wealth to keep up with the new plutocracy. Given this constraint, the exclusive expressive domains of the Córdoba plutocracy that are beyond the reach of the upper middle class are those that demand a great deal of money, that is, disposable incomes of $1 million a year or more. Focusing on first-rank plutocrats (particularly those with fortunes of more than $100 million), they are first in various domains of local conspicuous consumption (ostentatious mansions equipped with the most up-to-date surveillance and service gadgetry and a fixation with technology ranging from cars and planes to sound and visual systems). More out of reach of the upper middle class, and even second-rank plutocrats, are expressive domains realized abroad, the most notable being traveling in the grand style for months at a time and establishing palatial residences in the border states. The latter is a trend that started modestly in the early 1970s and has now become the rage and a source of competition among the richest plutocrats; the value of these residences ranges from $15 million to $20 million. It should be noted, however, that more modest plutocrats, many politicians, and considerable numbers of the more affluent upper middle class have residences in the border states. Parenthetically, many rich and powerful Mexicans today have residences in the United States, which stems from a sense of social and economic insecurity that affluent Mexicans have felt during the past generation.

In all other respects, Córdoba's superordinately placed share essentially the same expressive array. There are a few exceptions: some expressive domains are exclusive of particular groups of the superordinately placed. Two examples illustrate this anomaly. First, the political class departs significantly from the plutocracy and to some extent from the well-established upper middle class. With respect to the former, even the wealthiest politicians, after a career in local high office, do not usually become plutocrats, that is, engage in some entrepreneurial activity generating more wealth. This is quite the opposite on the national level, where invariably successful politicians become high-flown plutocrats. I explain this difference in terms of the larger fortunes that national politicians amass while in office. Thus even the rare regional politician who amasses a fortune comparable to second-rank plutocrats does not engage in any form of local conspicuous consumption, let alone the extravagances of expression realized abroad. Rather, after retiring from office, politicians generally maintain a low profile, primarily to avoid undue scrutiny and criticism, which is much more likely to happen in the rather close environment of a provincial city.

Second, the traditional upper middle class stands apart from the new upper middle class; the former constitutes the local upper class, characterized by several exclusive expressive domains. With its own lineage and traditions of long standing and close relationship with the former hacendado class, the traditional upper middle class today continues to function as a model for the rank-and-file upper middle class. The domains of expression that they embody include household decoration and display, "proper" ways to entertain, a taste for fine furniture and antiques, and in general the niceties of "elegant" living, as dictated by local standards.[9]

The inclusive expressive array of Córdoba's superordinately placed includes a large ensemble of domains that encompasses all major ethnographic categories. Though my discussion must be limited to what is directly relevant to stratification and social mobility, a few generalizations are in order.

As far as I have investigated this matter, the size of the expressive array of Córdoba's superordinately placed is roughly constituted by 230 domains of realization, that is, about half the size of the expressive array of the aristocracy-plutocracy in Mexico City. (This is quite consonant with the fact—as I have tentatively established by computing the expressive arrays of the Mexican aristocracy, rural Tlaxcalans, and the Mapuche Indians of southern Chile—that the expressive array of a social group is directly proportional to its cultural complexity.) These domains exist in all major ethnographic categories, but the array is unevenly distributed. The ethnographic categories with the most expressive domains are material culture and technology, entertainment and recreation, and economics and economic life; those with fewest are religious organization and ritualism, kinship and social organization, and etiquette and protocol. In between are demography and race, hobbies and sports, and life and annual cycles.

The most conservative sector of the superordinately placed is the traditional upper middle class; its array is focused on religious organization and ritualism and etiquette and protocol, domains that are always more salient for groups that are no longer creating new forms of expression and for whom concern with lineage and the past betrays their reduced economic standing. The most innovative are plutocrats; their newly acquired wealth naturally leads them to create new domains of expression (in the local context, that is) in material culture and technology and economics and economic life. The vast majority of the superordinate sector, the upper middle class, insofar as its wealth permits it, try to emulate the plutocracy, do not in any sense innovate, and disregard the rearguard expressive involvements of the traditional upper middle class as largely useless. Finally, the small political class is expressively the poorest, due to its intent to be unnoticed, although it shares a large number of domains with the upper middle class, in whatever upwardly mobile aspirations individual members may have. I shall close with a comparison of provincial and national superordinate expression.

Before undertaking the comparison, it is necessary to analyze several analytical points that are implicit in the foregoing description. The first matter to take up is the significance of the endogenous realization of expression and its exogenous entailment and perception. Put differently, what are the functions of the manifold forms of expression, and how does their realization affect social mobility and class consciousness?

All types of expression that I have so far identified (natural, conflict, terminal, palliative, and vicarious) are differentially discharged and with various degrees of incidence by the components of Córdoba's superordinately placed. But the most intensely realized are natural, palliative, and vicarious expression. I have dealt extensively elsewhere (Nutini 2004, Chapter 1) with the structural significance of the various types of expression, and here I will briefly outline their main tenets in order to make the ongoing discussion fully intelligible.

Natural expression. Natural expression is a universal attribute of the cultural system of all classes and social groups; ignoring expression at the expense of structure leaves many aspects of social life unexplained, and this is particularly the case in the study of social stratification (see Chapter 1). The most characteristic attribute of natural expressive behavior is that the sociopsychological motivation for its realization is the same regardless of social class or ethnic affiliation.

Conflict expression. Conflict expressions are special kinds of behavior that are tied to changes in the social structure of such groups that are often associated with revolutions or situations of rapid change and individually with changes in socioeconomic standing, such as what has been happening throughout the entire spectrum of the stratification system of Mexico since the 1910 Revolution. Conflict expression is explained by Roberts and Sutton-Smith's (1962) conflict-enculturation theory of model involvement. More specifically, I described this form of expression in terms of the loss of wealth and economic power and, more recently, of social prestige and position, as a role model for the rising plutocracy, that the Mexican aristocracy has undergone in the twentieth century.

Terminal expression. Terminal expression takes place when a salient institution or social group of long standing is on the threshold of rapid change or demise; the actors, seeming to anticipate the eventual result, may exaggerate some customary structural discharge, which betrays a more expressive than instrumental component. Let me illustrate. As I construe it for the Mexican aristocrats enfranchised in Mexico City, terminal expression is really a syndrome that manifests itself as follows. Sensing that their group was in the last stage of social prominence and rapidly moving into irrelevance, aristocrats engaged in one last outburst of expressive realization, a renaissance of brilliant social activity from the early 1940s to the early 1950s, ending forever their undisputed social dominance. I have recorded the same syndrome in Córdoba's traditional upper middle class. Terminal expression, however, is realized in several social contexts.

Palliative expression. This expression usually takes place in social groups that are undergoing drastic transformations, and consequently it is closely related to terminal expression; individually, it is manifest when people are in difficult and painful predicaments. Again, as in the case of the Mexican aristocracy in its last stage as a functional group, palliative and terminal expression are regarded as contextually complementary but performing basically the same function, namely, assuaging the individual and collective pain of contemplating ultimate demise. Thus palliative expression embodies the individual mechanisms for the assuagement of pain, whereas terminal expression generates the social context of its realization.

Vicarious expression. Though I have discussed the most salient attributes of vicarious expression, a few more remarks are in order here. Vicarious expression is a form of natural expression, certainly one of its most universal variations, and particularly associated, at least in Western civilization, with social mobility along the entire spectrum of all stratification systems. As a concept, vicarious expression is, on the one hand, the centerpiece in understanding the relationship of structural-expressive realization between two proximate social classes; on the other hand, it suggests an explanation for social mobility in terms of the expressive needs that validate the acquisition of higher structural status. To put it differently, the concept has two main aspects, vicarious perception and vicarious attraction, which denote, respectively, how a class in the stratificational scale perceives another that is superordinately placed and what the latter has to offer that is desired by the former. Finally, one of the consequences of all forms of vicariousness is that it establishes a relationship of power and control of the superordinate over the subordinate.

How and by what specific groups in Córdoba's superordinately placed are these types of expression realized? Natural expression is evidently realized by all groups and, with the exceptions noted above, constitutes the inclusive array of the superordinately placed. It includes domains in all ethnographic categories but varies in the intensity of group realization. Fundamentally, the natural expressive array determines the class consciousness of the superordinately placed, the behavioral common denominator that identifies the class vis-à-vis all other classes in Córdoba's stratification system. To put it differently, class consciousness is to a significant extent configured by the visibility of behavior. Lest I may be misunderstood, the necessary conditions of class consciousness are most assuredly determined by structural factors (wealth, power, education), but its sufficient conditions are always expressive. In other words, what is immediately (directly) perceived about a social class is its expressive behavior, and this largely shapes the image it elicits from other social classes in the stratification system, even though in the present case it is the power and wealth of the superordinate class that determines its structural position.

Palliative expression is realized exclusively by the traditional upper middle class to assuage their loss of status as the arbiters of appropriate behavior. Finding themselves increasingly irrelevant, as no longer a model for either the plutocracy or the upper middle class, members of the traditional upper middle class have largely retreated by emphasizing lineage, tradition, and the glories of the past, a classic manifestation of palliative expression.

Much more significant is the realization of vicarious expression, or more precisely, expressive emulation. Above, I have implicitly assumed that expressive emulation underlies aspirations to upward mobility. Expressive emulation, however, accomplishes much more conceptually; that is, it is one of the main mechanisms of class mobility, and its function is the same throughout the stratificational spectrum. Let me amplify this point. The traditional standpoint on upward mobility is that exclusively structural factors, primarily education and the acquisition of wealth, propel individuals and groups to rise on the social scale. This is also true with respect to class mobility but only in the sense that structural factors constitute the necessary conditions of mobility; the sufficient conditions are expressive, without which the dynamics of mobility are not entirely understood. The immediate motivation is the perception of the expressive behavior of a higher class that the members of a lower class expect to emulate. The complementarity of structural and expressive factors is evident: expressive behaviors constitute the immediate psychological attraction, which are entailed by structural factors that determine the expressive behavior of the higher class that is being emulated. I will postpone the detailed analysis of social mobility until the description of how it is realized in the other classes of Córdoba's stratification system. In the conclusion, I discuss all the ramifications of the combined structural expressive approach, which should result in a limited-range theory of social class and mobility.

Finally, I want to compare the expressive arrays of the superordinate classes in Córdoba and Mexico City. The main object of the comparison is to establish differences and similarities between the expressive cultures of the superordinately placed in Córdoba and in Mexico City. Moreover, the comparison should be instructive for assessing the provincial and the national stratification system.

First, I want to reiterate that the superordinate stratification systems of Córdoba and Mexico City entail the same categories: a dying aristocracy, a plutocracy, a political class, and an upper middle class. There is one exception; there never was a sufficiently large aristocratic hacendado class in the Córdoba region to speak of a local aristocracy.[10] The closest to it is the traditional upper middle class, which in close social contact with the hacendados and by virtue of their own lineage and local history, influenced the expressive life of the local superordinately placed from an aristocratic perspective. In all other respects, these two stratification systems are structurally equivalent.

What are the specific expressive similarities? The conceptual and dynamic aspects of expression are the same, and all the types of expression have the equal functions in the two systems. Three examples should clarify the matter. First, before I began the systematic investigation of Córdoba's stratification system (summer 1992), I predicted that the expressive array of the superordinately placed would be significantly smaller. My prediction was correct; it is about half of the array of the superordinately placed in Mexico City. This is a clear indication that the same principles are at work, as the extent of the expressive array of a social class is a function of size and complexity. Second, assuming that Córdoba's traditional upper middle class is structurally equivalent to the aristocracy in Mexico City, vicarious emulation proceeds in the same fashion in the two situations. Just as in the case of the national plutocracy's expressive emulation of the aristocracy during its period of gestation and maturation (late 1920s to late 1980s), the local plutocracy learns and internalizes (early 1940s to early 1990s), secondhand from the traditional upper middle class, the basic aristocratic domains of behavior so as to validate the new social status that the acquisition of great wealth and power demands.[11] This form of emulation, though in a more subdued form, has affected the upper middle class as well, particularly in its role as a support social group to the plutocracy. Third, the aristocracy in Mexico City and its surrogate, the traditional upper middle class in Córdoba, after having fulfilled their role as the expressive model for the superordinately placed, are rapidly disappearing as functionally distinct social classes in the superordinately placed sectors of their respective societies. The increasing irrelevance of a social class that has survived mainly as an expressive model for the rich and powerful, is an unmistakable indication that the stratification system of Mexico is evolving: from a system in which expressive factors (lineage, appropriate behavior, tradition, concern with the past, etc.) are significant in social class formation to a system in which structural factors (power, wealth, education, occupation, etc.) are the sole determinants of class membership. This is what has been happening to the Mexican stratification system everywhere, from top to bottom. In other words, the Mexican system is becoming more and more like that of modern industrial nations, and what has retarded it are primarily economic factors, particularly the lack of job opportunities.

Moving on to the differences, these are centered exclusively on the empirical (ethnographic) content of domains in the expressive array. I have already mentioned a very important one — that the size of the array of Córdoba's superordinately placed is about half that of Mexico City's superordinately placed. Just as significant, the "quality" and "sophistication" of the latter's array are significantly greater than those of the former's. In a nutshell, the expressive culture of the elite of Córdoba is a poor cousin to that of Mexico City, and this entails more than the natural differences between center and periphery. Rather, they are due mostly to two factors: the absence of a direct expressive influence of the aristocracy on Córdoba's plutocracy and the latter's source of emulation derived mostly from foreign plutocratic origins. Again, it would take an entire chapter to do justice to this problem, but I must limit myself to a few examples.

Kinship, religion, and concern with the past are fertile domains of expressive realization among aristocrats, some of which, by a process of expressive acculturation, have been internalized by the national plutocracy. None of these domains are expressively significant for Córdoba's plutocracy and upper middle class. Rather, as I have indicated, the core of the local array is material culture and technology, which the expressive life of the plutocracy extensively realizes, the upper middle class tries to emulate, and the traditional upper middle class cannot afford. Indeed, material culture and technology, derived primarily from foreign plutocratic models, are the domains in which the local plutocracy is creating its own expressive array.

Collecting, fine cuisine, decoration and display, and etiquette and protocol are diagnostic domains of the acculturative expressive array that has emerged among the superordinately placed in Mexico City; they are conspicuously absent among the superordinately placed in Córdoba. As they are of aristocratic derivation, one would not expect to find them in Córdoba, except in an attenuated form among the traditional upper middle class. To specify, collecting is confined to cars and other technological objects; there is no interest in collecting the paintings, antique furniture, pre-Hispanic objects, and other fine arts that grace most superordinately placed houses in Mexico City. The traditional Mexican haute cuisine, in which aristocratic households excel, is nonexistent; in all fairness, it would be surprising if it were otherwise, since this art has almost disappeared from Mexican culture. There is none of the great care and concern with decoration and display that characterizes most superordinately placed households in Mexico City; the local household may contain very expensive decorative items, but it rarely has the elegance of the former. The local superordinate classes are an informal, folksy social set that scorns etiquette and protocol; again, however, the traditional upper middle class is the exception: to some extent it has preserved various aspects of the social life of the old hacendado families.

In conclusion, the conceptual similarity between the organization of the arrays of the superordinately placed in Córdoba and Mexico City demonstrates the cross-societal validity of expressive factors as a complement to structural factors in the study of class formation and mobility, whereas differences in the empirical compositions of the expressive arrays of these two elite contexts illustrate variations in realization due to isolation and sources of emulation. The foregoing analysis also applies largely to the expressive arrays of the middle class, the working class, and the dispossessed.

Chapter 4 | THE MIDDLE STRATUM

*The Middle and Lower Middle Classes
and the Working Class*

The middle stratum in Mexican society everywhere is the most difficult to visualize, to break down into subclasses, and to analyze structurally and expressively. This is certainly the case in the Córdoba region, as well as in the most affluent regions of the country and the great urban centers. One could say that the three subclasses that are isolated and analyzed in this chapter—the middle class, the lower middle class, and the working class—are approximations of the U.S. class system as described by sociologists. One of the aims of this chapter is to determine the differences and similarities of the stratification of Córdoba and of the United States, as Mexico has evolved during the past two generations. Moreover, the rationale for grouping these distinct subclasses into a middle stratum is that social mobility here is greater than any other along the range of the regional stratification system. To treat these subclasses separately would detract from understanding the mechanism of class mobility, particularly what this process means when the offspring of working-class parents enter the middle class.

THE MIDDLE STRATUM IN STRUCTURAL PERSPECTIVE

Until the Revolution of 1910, Mexico was a two-class system: the superordinate sector and the dominated masses. This situation was mediated by a small middle class of merchants and professionals. As a result primarily of more educational opportunities and Mexico's industrial growth, there has been considerable social mobility, which has increased the ranks of the middle classes.

The difficulty of conceptualizing the middle stratum of society in Córdoba and the region has to do with the rapid mobility from the ranks of the dispossessed into the lower middle and working classes, on the one hand, and the generational mobility from the lower middle class into the middle class, on the other. For the former, the process of class formation has been complicated by the need for physical mobility. The overwhelming majority of the dispossessed are rural folk, few of whom can attain working-class status in their native communities; thus they move to urban areas, in this case, almost exclusively to Córdoba. Thus the dispossessed in Córdoba are not a product of the city itself but are labor migrants from rural communities.[1] However, the five small cities of the region spawn a significant number of dispossessed folk, which is also the result of permanent migration from nearby rural communities. There is seldom outward migration once people settle in these small cities, and most of those who do migrate to Mexico City or other large urban centers in Mexico are from rural communities. The same obtains in Córdoba, which is the final migratory destination of people from the region. Moreover, Cordobeses along the entire stratification spectrum seldom migrate out of the region.

The absence of geographic mobility by itself in all urban centers of the region affects vertical, generational mobility. What I wish to convey is that movement up to the middle class is achieved primarily by the sons and daughters of working- and lower-middle-class people who, through hard work and perseverance, provide for their children's university educations (mostly in law, medicine, engineering, chemistry, veterinary medicine, economics, business administration, accounting, and primary and secondary education), which launches them into professions or small business enterprises as the first step into a middle-class existence. Inhabiting the same urban environments, sometimes living in close proximity, it is difficult to determine the class position of the younger descending generation with respect to their parents', which is most clearly manifested in their expressive culture.

The most significant structural consequence of mobility from the working and lower middle classes into the middle class is a distinct lack of class consciousness. In no domain is this more noticeable than in differences of expressive behavior. Whereas the three main rungs of the superordinate class, as discussed in Chapter 3, have a clear conception of who they are and can verbalize their position in society, the middle classes have a vague notion of the middle position they occupy. When they are asked to what social class they belong, members of the three "social classes" that for analytical purposes I have isolated in this chapter answer, with notable exceptions, that they are "middle class," irrespective of the work they do and the functions they perform in society.[2] In other words, the etic conception of class and mobility in the middle stratum, on which this book is based, is a more accurate reflection of the emic reality than of what the actors of the social system are consciously aware. This is a situation that I encountered many times in the various ethnographic domains on my work in central Mexico.

There is an even more pronounced ideological and expressive distinction between "white-collar" and "blue-collar" workers, as these terms are used by sociologists in the United States. They correspond roughly to the lower middle class and the working class, as these terms are used here, but entail notable differences. They are underlain by education and earning power but more significantly determined by the traditional Mexican syndrome that those who do manual work do not command as much respect and rank lower in the social scale than those who do not. This aspect of the worldview of Mestizo Mexico everywhere is expressed in many ways, and we decided to test it in the study of Córdoba and the region. Indeed, more than ethnicity (defined as Indian or Mestizo status in the rural context, and in the passage from rural to urban existence, a cultural transition that always carries racial connotations) this syndrome plays an important role in people's perception of stratification, which is another complicating factor in bridging the emic and etic conception of class and mobility.

Finally, I would like to reiterate the role of expression in the etic categorization of class. It is even more determinant in the middle stratum than in the superordinate stratum in isolating and determining the interaction among its component subclasses. As I have already indicated, the expressive and behavioral components of class are always more visible than its structural components. This is magnified in the rapid formation of the middle stratum during the past two generations, which leads me to justify describing and analyzing together its structurally quite different subclasses.

Essentially the task of this chapter is to give an etic account of the emic perceptions of class of this disparate sector of the stratification of Córdoba and the region. I came to the conclusion that the people's emic perceptions were significantly at variance with the etic classification that warranted best the description of the facts. Moreover, the three subclasses must be described and analyzed as a whole, lest our understanding of the dynamics of social mobility from the lower middle and working class would be compromised. Thus, after describing the three subclasses of the middle stratum, I shall analyze the factors and contexts that determine social mobility.

THE MIDDLE STRATUM | 83

THE SOLID MIDDLE CLASS

The solid middle class (SMC), as a distinct sector of the middle stratum, is rather small, probably less than 15 percent of the total population of Córdoba and the region. It comprises a varied group of professionals (mostly physicians, lawyers, engineers, architects, dentists, accountants, and agronomists), medium-size businessmen (owners of retail stores, specialty stores, laboratories, small health clinics, contractors, and several other categories of service establishments), farmers and ranchers, midlevel bank officials, and bureaucrats in the local, state, and federal governments.[3] Most of the families of these businessmen and professionals have been SMC for at least a generation, some for two or three generations. The most distinguished professionals and the owners of many retail stores and service concerns are well known to the people at large, and their offices and establishments are part of the geographic and business gestalt of the city of Córdoba. It should be noted, however, that about 20 percent of these SMC families reside in the other cities of the region, particularly Fortin.

The economic affluence of the SMC is considerable, but it varies significantly among the component sectors.[4] The highest incomes of the SMC are earned by businessmen and farmers. I was unable to establish with certainty the gross income per year derived from their businesses and other enterprises, but I can estimate that it ranges from $75,000 to $150,000, and in a few cases (those who own two or three retail and service enterprises) incomes may be as high as those of the upper middle class. The affluence of the families in this sector of the SMC permits them to live in well-appointed houses with three or four bedrooms, quite often in the elite residential sections of Córdoba, to own two or three automobiles, and to send their children to the best schools in Mexico City. That they can afford one or two maids and other imponderables makes it difficult to distinguish them from upper-middle-class families; and compared to solid middle-class families in the United States, they probably enjoy a higher standard of living. The comparison, however, shrinks to insignificance when one realizes that SMC families in Córdoba constitute a small percentage of the population, whereas American middle-class families constitute the majority of the population in any comparable unit.

The professional sector ranks below that of businessmen and entrepreneurs in economic affluence but higher in intrinsic prestige in the perception of class. The professions themselves are ranked in prestige as follows: medicine, architecture, engineering, agronomy, accounting, law, and dentistry.[5] In terms of earning power, lawyers rank at the top, followed by physicians, accountants, dentists, engineers, architects, and agronomists. It is a difficult task to determine with certainty the gross income of these professionals. The problem is complicated by the fact that most of them are self-employed or work for private concerns and government agencies at fixed salaries. The situation is further complicated by the relative prestige of the university or college that granted their degrees and the specialization practiced by professionals. After estimating the ranges of income characteristic of each profession, I will discuss the complicating factors.

Individual lawyers earn the highest incomes but also have the greatest range of variation. Lawyers with degrees from local state universities, having small practices, or working for private concerns or government agencies are the lowest earners, with gross incomes of less than $35,000 a year. At the opposite extreme, lawyers with degrees from the National University of Mexico and other prestigious law schools in the capital may earn incomes of more than $150,000 a year, particularly when they own a public notary office. Much the same obtains with physicians, except that the range of salaries is narrower: $30,000 to $120,000 per year, depending on specialty and length of practice. All other professionals have considerably less income per year and seldom make more than $80,000; a considerable number make less than $30,000. The least well paid of the SMC are midlevel bank personnel and bureaucrats, whose salaries range from $15,000 to $40,000 per year.

Tax evasion is rampant among the superordinate classes and the SMC; in extent and intensity it is greater in the former than in the latter. I was unable to get an accurate picture of this endemic practice in the superordinate classes (essentially the complicated system of bribery and legal maneuvering that goes with it), and that is why I did not discuss it in the previous chapter. However, I was able to obtain the general characteristic of this practice among the SMC, which is simpler and does not usually involve legal stratagems. It takes the following forms: among professionals, the most common practice is not giving receipts and not entering services rendered into accounting books; among businessmen of all sorts, by bribing with the connivance of local, state, and federal tax-collecting officials and occasionally by falsifying records; among farmers (especially sugar and coffee planters), by underreporting production or selling without receipts and by other subtler illegal procedures. As much as 40 percent of gross income may not be reported, meaning that the tax evaders are nearly doubling their disposable income. Given that about 60 percent of the population (the dispossessed and considerable numbers of the working class) do not pay income tax, one can see how difficult it is for the government to raise revenues. Because this problem exists everywhere in Mexico, the government is unable to generate enough revenues to improve the economic and health conditions of the poor.

All professionals have university degrees and are therefore the best trained, but this does not mean they are the best educated. It is often the case that the most educated (in the liberal sense of the term) are businessmen and bureaucrats, who may have only a high school education or one or two years of college. This results in differences in expressive realization, as I discuss below. Intrinsically, the most prestigious professionals are graduates from the Universidad Nacional Autónoma de México, the Instituto Tecnológico de Monterrey, the Universidad Iberoamericana, and a few other elite schools. Most of them, however, are graduates from local (Veracruz) universities, and a few have pursued graduate studies in the United States. What this pecking order essentially means is that, all things being equal, the more prestigious the university, the greater the income.

Ethnically, the majority of the SMC is of Mestizo extraction, mostly light phenotypically but including a significant number of Caucasoid and a wide range of Indian-Negroid phenotypes. As in most regions in Mexico, the higher you go in the social-economic scale, the higher the incidence of European phenotypes. Racial considerations, or rather phenotypic perceptions, do not play a determinant role in interclass relationships, but individuals do engage in the cultural whitening syndrome when it allows them to maximize economic and social ends. Race, in other words, plays a small role in self-perception of the SMC, except that it is quite common for the majority to regard themselves as criollos. From a different perspective, the reason phenotypic traits do not play a determinant role in defining class membership is that the degree of Mestizoization is difficult to categorize. Individually, however, phenotypic traits are significantly manipulated in upward social mobility and in maximizing economic ends. (The general rule in the Mexican stratification system everywhere is that the manipulation of phenotypic traits — or the whitening syndrome — increases from the bottom to the top.)

Another constant that I have observed in the Mexican stratification system is that the higher the social mobility into another social class, the higher the class consciousness. (This may be a universal characteristic of all stratification systems.) The SMC, in contrast to the other two subclasses in the middle stratum, is the most class conscious, whereas the working and lower classes do not exhibit a collective perception of occupying a well-defined niche in society or a sense of belonging to a clearly defined social or economic group. The SMC readily verbalizes who they are and their role in society, emphasizing the admitted conceit that they are the cogs that make the machine of society work—through their own efforts and without the dishonesty and illicit behavior of the rich and powerful. I heard this, and similar overblown comments, from many SMC informants, which, regardless of whether they are true, attest to their economic class consciousness. When it comes to social and political action, however, their class consciousness is greatly diminished. The SMC seldom engages in concerted efforts to benefit the community or, politically, to curtail the high-handedness and outright abuses of the rich and powerful.

Given their substantial membership, formal education, technical knowledge, and wealth, the SMC is in an enviable position to influence regional events. Yet the perception of members of the SMC that they are the sector of society that makes things work is largely empty: they have never managed to organize to promote the welfare and defend the rights of the underclasses; they seldom engage in charity work; and rather than try to counteract corruption, they ignore it. They regard their role in society as sufficient justification for the economic role they play.[6] Of all the distinct classes that make up the regional stratification system, the SMC is the least engaged and the most isolated socially, politically, and economically from the bulk of the people. This is a difficult phenomenon to understand, since on the whole SMC people, by the very nature of their activities, are physically in rather intimate contact with the rest of society.

Residentially, the SMC is rather indistinguishable from the upper middle class. Whether in Córdoba or in the five small cities of the region (where a rather small percentage of families are enfranchised), SMC families live in close physical proximity to upper-middle-class families, usually in the elite areas. Under such circumstances, the SMC (in particular, the most affluent businessmen and distinguished professionals) and upper-middle-class families frequently interact socially, occasionally leading to matrimonial alliances. Some SMC families also have country retreats; this and other expressive practices tend to blur the distinction between the SMC and the upper middle class.

The SMC is probably the least religious of all distinct classes of the regional stratification system: they are the least likely to attend church, they are not close to their parishes, and they are the least traditional in celebrating most of the religious events of the year. SMC families are overwhelmingly Catholic; there are no Protestants, a few Muslims, and three Jewish families. As far as I am aware, no SMC people have converted to evanagelical Protestantism in more than sixty years of increasing proselytism. The reasons are twofold. First, as the least religious sector of the population, the SMC is not about to convert, and conversion to evangelical Protestantism is considered a lower- and lower-middle-class phenomenon. Second, members of the SMC do not need the social and economic support that evangelical Protestant sects provide.

The SMC's kinship system is basically the same as that of the upper middle class, except that the incidence of the bifocal extended family is higher. It is not a permanent form of residence, but as in countless societies (tribal, folk, and modern) throughout the world, it is a way to help married couples get on their feet economically before establishing neo-local households. The wider social organization of the SMC also differs from the upper middle class in having closer ties among the households of sliding kindreds and a significantly larger network of compadrazgo ties. With respect to the former, the patrilateral-matrilateral kin is structured by nonkinship variables, such as the affluence of certain households, that attract significant numbers of younger households and households of distinguished individuals and consolidate significant numbers of couples, making the kindred a more operational kinship unit. With respect to the latter, SMC couples contract more than twice as many types of compadrazgo as the three subclasses of the superordinate class. Superordinate compadrazgo is confined essentially to sacramental types (baptism, confirmation, first communion, and marriage), which are always symmetrically discharged, except when politicians and occasionally plutocrats, for political and economic reasons respectively, engage in public-collective compadrazgo types, such as sponsoring (*apadrinar*) an entire high school graduating class. SMC families contract all sacramental types plus several other compadrazgo types: graduation (from grammar school, high school, college, etc.), silver wedding anniversary, *quinceaños* (celebration of a girl's fifteenth birthday), *primera piedra* (setting the foundations of a house), and so on. The resulting compadrazgo networks have significant social and some economic importance, whereas among the superordinately placed, compadrazgo is confined to the immediate rites and ceremonies and seldom entail social and economic responsibilities.

There is a significant degree of mobility from the SMC to the upper middle class, particularly among the most distinguished professionals and agricultural entrepreneurs. Indeed, it was quite evident that during the five years of the data-gathering process for this study (1993–1998), there was a significant number of SMC families in transition to upper-middle-class status. This process of upward mobility may be described as follows. It begins when an SMC individual and his family seek to establish social relations with a specific upper-middle-class family (usually by inviting the couple to a cocktail or dinner party) with whom they have been distantly friendly or have had business contacts, and frequently when their children attend the same school. If the invitation is reciprocated, it is a sure sign of acceptance and usually leads to a permanent relationship. The second step is taken by the upper-middle-class family in generating acceptance for the SMC family, which may take a variety of forms: invitations to important events in the life or annual cycle, introducing the SMC couple to prominent upper-middle-class families, and in general facilitating interaction of the SMC couple and their children with their upper-middle-class counterparts. Quite often, after the SMC family has been well accepted in the new social milieu, matrimonial alliances follow, which may be regarded as the final step in the process of incorporation. From beginning to end, the process may take from as few as five years to as many as fifteen years. The most notable changes that take place in the process of upward mobility are expressive, and they are described below.

Expressive Analysis

SMC individuals and families are consumed with material concerns, to get ahead economically and to avoid at all cost and in any respect of going down in the social scale. More than any other social class in the stratification system, the SMC is concerned with making sufficient money to satisfy vicarious modes of expression that they observe directly from the upper middle class and indirectly from television, newspapers, and magazines and limited travel outside Mexico, primarily to the border states of the United States. Thus the SMC, as the most upwardly mobile sector of society, engage almost exclusively in natural and vicarious forms of expression. The former constitutes mostly the inclusive array (including sports, many forms of entertainment, and many other domains of expression associated with urban living), which in different degrees they share with other classes of the stratification system. The latter is underlain by the vicariousness that always accompanies the upwardly mobile, and its main purveyor in situ is the upper middle class. It should be clarified that not all SMC families are upwardly mobile; many are quite satisfied with their position in society, do not necessarily strive to keep up with the Joneses, do not aspire to become upper middle class, and so do not engage in vicarious expression. I do not know what percentage of SMC families is in this category, but I do know that it is a minority. As this is a study of stratification, I will dispense with natural expression and concentrate on vicarious expression and its relationship to upward mobility.

Vicarious expression among the SMC is centered on the household, home decoration, dressing, personal demeanor, proper speech, and public comportment. While the realization of this diversified array, involving many domains of expression, may be influenced by what they see on television and read in print, the immediate input is what they directly observe or imagine upper middle class people do. This strategy does not always produce the intended results. SMC families must be careful not to try too hard to be accepted, which may rather result in rejection. Those families who play the game of upward mobility well are quickly accepted, those who do not may take much longer, and some will never be accepted. After three or four years of trying, rejected families turn vociferously egalitarian, spending precious economic resources to promote a more just social system. (This is another form of expression that is more the result of sour grapes than conviction.)

As in the case of the upper middle class, the vicarious emulation that accompanies upward mobility is most effectively realized in the most visible domains of expression after an SMC family consciously embarks on the process of upward mobility. Of course, an upper-middle-class family does not begin this concerted effort until it has achieved the required economic position: a house in an elite section of Córdoba or Fortin (SMC families in the other four small cities of the region seldom aspire to become upper middle class unless they establish residence in these two cities), all the material symbols of affluence (cars, the best household appliances, children attending the best local schools), and so on. Thus the prelude to the onset of conscious upward mobility may involve years of hard work.

It is the wife of a successful SMC professional, rancher, or businessman who suggests an overt campaign of upward mobility after she has been exposed, albeit superficially, to upper-middle-class behavior in the context of social, religious, or entertainment events. If the husband agrees, which is most often the case, a specific strategy is agreed on. If the couple does not live in an elite section of Córdoba or Fortin, the first order of business is to buy a house there or, preferably, have one built. Four or five architects in Córdoba build houses for the superordinate classes, and they usually manage to convince the couple that the appropriate house is one that is in the style they have built many times, knowing full well the couple's intentions. The result is usually one more blemish on the cityscape.

Acquiring the appropriate house is easy compared to the task of outfitting it with the proper accoutrements: furniture, accessories (rugs, curtains, lamps, etc.), and art (paintings, watercolors, sculptures, etc.). Although there are two interior decoration businesses in Córdoba, the most successful upwardly mobile SMC families go to Mexico City and, with the help of a well-established interior decorator, buy what is required; they may even bring this interior decorator to their homes in Córdoba or Fortin to complete the job. This can be an expensive and sometimes risky proposition, as interior decorators usually charge exorbitant fees and also try to sell the kitchy items that they cannot dispose of in Mexico City. In the game of upward mobility, however, a gaudily decorated SMC house may not necessarily be a drawback, as many in the upper middle class may have suffered equally in their attempts to keep up with the Joneses.

Coterminous with the couple building or acquiring a new house and decorating it, the wife, especially, practices what she has observed of upper-middle-class dress, patterns of speech, and personal demeanor. They also systematically inform themselves, by reading and watching television, about what they perceive is appropriate behavior. The last step in this period of expressive learning, which may last two or more years, culminates in approaching an upper-middle-class family or families with whom they have been superficially associated. The initial step is an invitation to a specially orchestrated household event, the main object of which is to demonstrate that they run a proper household and that they behave as well as those whom they are trying to emulate. If preliminary acceptance is the outcome of the initial personal encounter, there are too many imponderables to assess the course of the process at the end of which the SMC family may be said to have become upper middle class. Among these imponderables are the ability of the SMC family to play the game of emulation, the creativity it exhibits in social and personal behavior, and the initiative to undertake actions that are pleasing to the new class members. It may be five or six years before the SMC family considers itself and is perceived as upper middle class. In other words, at this juncture, as in all cases from the bottom to the top of the stratification system, mobility entails both an actual component and a perceived component of belonging to a higher social class.

The process of expressive emulation from the SMC to the upper middle class is always accompanied by the whitening syndrome, most assiduously among those individuals who depart the most from Caucasoid phenotypes. As is the case in the realization of the whitening syndrome, it has two components: the social and physical manipulations of the upwardly mobile to be perceived as more Caucasoid than they are; and the actions of the class members to which they aspire to facilitate this perception. With minor deviations and varying intensity, the realization of the whitening syndrome in the context of SMC upward mobility is the same as in the superordinate stratum, for example, when important politicians who are phenotypically Mestizo are incorporated into plutocratic and traditional upper-middle-class social circles. The expressive array of the SMC is, of course, much more extensive, but the domains discussed here are sufficient to understand the role of expressive emulation in SMC upward mobility.

THE LOWER MIDDLE AND WORKING CLASSES

There are few perceptible distinctions between the lower middle class and the working class, and describing them separately would create emic distinctions that would obfuscate the analysis. The differences are more expressive than structural, and they are noted in the section on expressive analysis. More significant is the deep-rooted distinction between white-collar and blue-collar families and families of the self-employed and salaried workers (*asalariados*).

The distinction between white- and blue-collar individuals and families bears close examination and entails structural implications that go beyond those that the same distinction has for social stratification in the United States. As discussed previously, this distinction is perhaps rooted in the traditional Spanish view that those who do manual work rank lower than those who do not. This, of course, is an ideological distinction that defies rationalization. Yet this belief prevails in the stratification system of Mexico; invariably a low-paid secretary is ranked higher socially than a well-paid factory worker who has the same education.

Thus, in the process of upward mobility, married couples want their children to become office workers and bank clerks rather than factory workers or mechanics. Although there are few structural differences between white- and blue-collar workers, the ideological shadow of the superordination of the former is always present in the strategies of upward mobility of lower- and working-class people.

Another complicating factor in the categorization of the lower and working classes is that of the self-employed, namely, the owners of the many small shops that characterize underdeveloped countries. This category includes not only the service businesses still present in industrial countries (e.g., barber shops, beauty shops, cleaners) but also all kinds of small shopkeepers and providers of multiple services.

It is difficult to estimate the strength of these two classes of the middle stratum. My guess is that the lower middle class is significantly weaker than the working class; the former constitutes about 20 percent and the latter slightly less than 30 percent of the total population. I think my estimate is correct, and these two subclasses constitute about 50 percent of the region's population.

Who constitutes the lower middle and working classes, and how do they correlate with the white-collar/blue-collar and self-employed/ salaried distinctions? The answers to these questions are etic constructions; that is, they are not overtly expressed by the people but are structurally and behaviorally part of the social stratification of the region.

The lower middle class ranks higher than the working class by virtue of being composed primarily of white-collar workers, with a small number of blue-collar workers. The latter are manual laborers but may also own their own businesses such as electrical and automotive mechanic shops. Moreover, all the salaried workers belong to the working class; that is, they do independent manual work or work for factories or the largest shops owned by members of the lower middle class. For example, there are many carpenters, masons, electricians, seamstresses, beauticians, and so on, who work independently and may be called to private residences to perform their trades, but there are more who work on-site at specific places of business or who are sent by these places of business to private residences to do a specific job. The owner of the shop may do manual work himself, but the fact that he owns the shop puts him in a higher rank in the social scale.

The lower middle class, then, is composed of the following categories of individuals and their nuclear families (it is important to specify this, as I will discuss below): schoolteachers (grammar, middle, and high school); instructors in technical schools (secretarial, practical nursing, accounting, etc.); mid- and lower-level local, state, and federal bureaucrats, including secretarial personnel; mid- and lower-level banking personnel; registered nurses; hospital technical personnel; independent lab operators; secretaries and receptionists in doctors', dentists', lawyers', insurance, and all other professional offices; clerks employed by large stores of various kinds; owners of small restaurants, diners, ice-cream parlors, hardware stores, bookstores, bakeries, bars, apothecaries (*boticas*), dry cleaners, and tanneries; tortilla, sandwich, taco, pastry, pizza, beauty, notions (*mercerías*), butcher, fish, flower, curio, jewelry, glass-cutting, locksmith, cigar-making, saddlery and leather, and upholstery, and other kinds of shops; owners of small automotive shops specializing in the repair of cars and trucks, body work, tire repair and alignment, mufflers, and so on; owners of repair shops, primarily electrical appliances, radio and television sets, bicycles, motorcycles, agricultural equipment, and hydraulic equipment; owners of video and Internet kiosks; and last and most numerous, owners of small convenience stores (popularly known as *misceláneas* or *changarros*) selling canned goods, soda pop, fruits, vegetables, and miscellaneous items for household consumption (they are ubiquitous in all villages, towns, and cities of the region and in the poor wards of Córdoba).

The working class is composed of the following categories of individuals and their nuclear families: factory workers in foundries, sugar mills, coffee mills, breweries, poultry farms; metallurgical, automotive parts, agricultural machinery, textiles, and paper-making factories; rice-processing, comestible oil making, soft drinks, food processing, cement, chemical, and fertilizer plants, and a few others; taxi drivers, bus drivers (both local and interstate), and agricultural machinery operators; cooks in large restaurants and fast-food places, bartenders, and waiters in restaurants and catering services; railroad and road workers; handymen and specialized workers employed by the cities; carpenters, masons, electricians, plumbers, mechanics, and other craftsmen working independently or employed by the shops; repair shops and other concerns mentioned in the foregoing paragraph; miscellaneous craftsmen working for the cities; specialized craftsmen, such as cabinetmakers and furniture makers, working independently or hired by established shops; and traditional midwives (*comadronas*), curers, and herbalists.

Ethnically, the lower middle and working classes are overwhelmingly Mestizo (included in this category is a strong mulatto component), with a few criollos, as characterized above, and a sprinkling of Europeans.

These two categories do not amount to more than 2 percent of the combined membership of the lower middle and working classes. To some extent they are anomalies, and they are often regarded by their more affluent counterparts in the SMC and the upper middle class as "losers." This is another form of racism that implies that criollos and individuals of European extraction should not have such status in society, particularly those doing blue-collar work.

What makes the depiction of the racial composition of the region difficult is the Negroid admixture. On the whole, the population in Córdoba and the region is significantly darker than in the average region of the highland; there are no entirely black communities, as I indicated above, but considerable numbers of people, mostly in the cities and a few communities in the lowlands (below 600 meters elevation), exhibit distinct Negroid features. Gradations of Mestizo and Mulatto populations (in villages and city wards) vary significantly, and it would be a hopeless task to attempt to specify, especially since phenotypical differences entail few direct sociological implications. Nonetheless, people are aware of phenotypical differences, and there is a certain degree of racism, particularly toward those exhibiting strong Negroid phenotypical traits.

The whitening syndrome has limited incidence among the lower middle and working classes. It takes place mainly among the most upwardly mobile families in the process of becoming SMC, including primarily two categories of families: the most successful owners of small stores, shops, restaurants, and other places of business and bureaucrats in government and the private sector on the way to managerial positions; and less often, blue-collar workers, particularly specialized artisans and factory workers (on the whole the best-paid working-class people). The former, given the nature of their occupations, interact closely with SMC individuals and families, which is the immediate stimulus for upward mobility. This situation is propitious for economic interaction to develop into mild social interaction, the next step of which is emulation. In the case of the latter, by dint of sacrifice, some blue-collar families manage to put some of their children through college, and this constitutes the initial conditions for upward mobility. This is a kind of generational mobility in which, at a given point in time, within the same nonresidential extended families, the nuclear families of parents and children may be engaged in significantly different expressive styles and be perceived as members of two subclasses of the middle stratum. The consequences of this more drastic, dual mobility is discussed in the expressive analysis.

It is under such conditions of upward mobility that the whitening syndrome quite often takes place, in the following fashions and domains. Lower-middle- and working-class people engage in the manipulation of phenotypic traits to conform to standards of beauty and demeanor that the national culture imposes on them. In other words, European standards of beauty and ideals of physical appearance play an important role in categorizing class and ethnicity. They provide models that people emulate to "improve" their physical appearance. For example, women forgo shaving their legs to enhance their European appearance and avoid wearing garments reminiscent of Indians. In emulating the SMC, men avoid marrying Indian-looking women to enhance their progeny's phenotypes and influence their children to do the same, often favoring their more European-looking offspring and neglecting the more Indian-looking ones. These are a few of the manipulations that lower-middle- and working-class people engage in the game of upward mobility. As stated previously, they are the result of the colonial mentality that still pervades many aspects of Mexican society.

In regard to affluence, there is a significant degree of variation in the categories of lower middle and working classes and in the way they make a living. First, all white- and blue-collar workers make at least twice the minimum salary (which for the region is 52 pesos—about $4.50 a day at the beginning of 2004, computed on a seven-day week). Second, almost invariably, blue-collar workers (particularly factory workers) are better remunerated than white-collar workers (especially store clerks and most banking personnel and secretaries and receptionists). Third, the salaries of primary and secondary school teachers amount to about the same as the wages of factory workers, while those of high school teachers are a little higher. Fourth, self-employed specialized craftsmen are better remunerated than those working for shops, repair shops, and other small concerns. Fifth, the owners of small concerns are by far the most affluent (a few of them with disposable incomes of tens of thousands of dollars), but it was practically impossible to obtain an accurate estimate of their affluence, due to their reticence to provide information, the size of their operations, and other factors. (The salaries and wages of most gainfully employed lower-middle- and working-class workers is a matter of public record; and the higher a researcher goes in the affluence scale, the less willing are people to talk about the money they earn).[7]

The following is a representative sample of the wages, salaries, and earnings of lower-middle and working class people, for the year 2000, computed in pesos.[8] (1) Grammar and secondary school teacher,

1,900–2,900; high school and technical school teachers, 3,000–4,200. (2) Bank clerks, 2,000–4,000 per month; office receptionists, 1,500–3,000; office secretaries, 1,000–2,000; store clerks, 900–1,500. (3) Factory workers (including sugar mill workers), 800–1,500 pesos per week. (4) Self-employed mechanics, carpenters, electricians, plumbers, masons, and other specialized workers, 3,500–5,500 per month. (5) Shop and repair shop owners, 80,000–120,000 pesos a year. (6) Owners of restaurants, stores, and other small business concerns, 150,000–350,000 per year. (The figures for categories 5 and 6 are rather rough estimates; those for the other categories are fairly accurate.)

How does this economic picture translate into the standard of living of the lower middle and working classes? With variations in elaborateness, most of the above categories of workers own homes or live in government-sponsored housing; very few live in apartment buildings. In the cities, outside the upscale sections inhabited by the rich and the SMC, the residences of the lower middle and working classes are located everywhere, in the periphery as well as in the midst of the commercial center. They are almost invariably equipped with gas stoves, refrigerators, television sets, and radios, and occasionally other household equipment. About 60 percent of working-class families own fifteen- to twenty-year-old cars, mostly American made, or more recent Volkswagen or Mitsubishi models; a smaller proportion of lower-middle-class families own more recent models; and the more affluent owners of their own businesses have bigger and more expensive cars. Other aspects of their material culture are discussed in the expressive analysis.

Most working-class people have finished elementary school, perhaps 30 percent have finished secondary school, and a few have some technical education. Lower-middle-class people are better educated, many have a high school education, and a few may have finished college or have a technical degree. Self-made men, with hardly any education, are among the most affluent store and shop owners, a common phenomenon along the entire spectrum of the stratification system. The average lower-middle- and working-class adult may be undereducated but invariably values education as an instrument of upward mobility and do their best to secure it for their children, sometimes at significant cost and deprivation.

Kinship, even among urbanites, is very important in building social and economic ties and in many respects retains some attributes of folk kinship in the general mentality of working-class people. The patrilaterally biased sliding kindred plays a significant role in organizing the social life of the people, sometimes approaching the efficacy of the unit in the folk situation; this is particularly the case among working-class people one generation or less from the folk context. With less residential proximity than in rural communities, the nonresidential extended family is also important and plays a significant role in the manifold life and annual events. The compadrazgo system is nearly as complex as the folk system; it includes all the types found among the SMC, plus several others, for a total of more than fifteen. Compadrazgo is always symmetrical, and as in the folk context, it extends most significantly beyond the immediate rites and ceremonies. Indeed, compadrazgo rivals kinship in generating social, economic, and religious resources.

Lower-middle- and working-class people are the most overtly Catholic of the urban stratificational spectrum, although their Catholicism is the least orthodox of all urbanites, as many of their practices are quite close to folk Catholicism. Traditional village ritual and ceremonialism permeates the discharge of many events in the life and annual cycles, which does not necessarily include going to confession and taking communion. At the same time lower-middle- and working-class people, particularly the latter, are the most dissatisfied with the church's inability to provide social and economic support, rendering them most vulnerable to evangelical Protestant proselytism.

Throughout the entire region in the past generation, Protestant evangelism has been successful in converting dissatisfied Catholics. It is difficult to estimate the percentage of converts, but a study now in progress suggests that perhaps as much as 25 percent of the lower middle and working classes has broken away from Catholicism. To give an idea of the spread of evangelism, one example suffices. In 1970 there was a single Protestant evangelist congregation in Fortin; by 1995 the number had increased to seven; and today Córdoba is regarded by local Catholic authorities as a hotbed of evangelism. The most active Protestant evangelist sects are the Jehovah's Witnesses, Pentecostals, Seventh-Day Adventists, and Mormons, which at the last count number more than two hundred rural and urban congregations.

A more recent development, within the past fifteen years, has been the proliferation of native evangelical sects. By this, I mean dissident movements away from Catholicism, doctrinally and pragmatically of American Protestant evangelist derivation. The Pentecostal and Jehovah's Witness sects are the most common sources of emulation, and native evangelical sects come into being in basically two ways. An individual or group, originally members of a Protestant sect, becomes dissatisfied with some organizational or doctrinal aspect, secedes, and launches a new movement;

or a divinely inspired leader initiates a native sect on hearing the word of God, who, in the time-honored Christian tradition, reveals to him the only true doctrinal path to worship him and provides the blue-print for the organization of the congregation. In reality, the new sect is a mélange of beliefs and practices of Protestant evangelical origin. In both cases, native evangelical sects quickly evolve and within a few years acquire their evangelical characteristics. Native evangelist sects consider themselves a Mexican movement away from Catholicism, and this nationalistic aspect is likely to grow, making native evangelism a formidable competitor of Protestant evangelism, as is already happening in several regions of central Mexico.

Both the lower middle class and the working class exhibit the least class consciousness of the middle stratum of society. The most affluent of the lower middle class, owners of the most successful stores and shops, quite often identify with the SMC, the first step toward that social status; but as a whole the lower middle class does not engage in characteristic social or economic action. The working class lacks just as much class consciousness, and there is little that unites, say, factory workers and specialized craftsmen, and the fact that they all do manual work does not translate into communal social or economic action to safeguard their interests in labor and other disputes.

The foregoing description and analysis applies primarily to the city of Córdoba and nearby Fortin, the urban hub of the region. This does not mean that there are no lower-middle-class and working-class people in the other less "sophisticated" cities or even in rural communities. Rather, the main difference between Córdoba-Fortin and the rest of the region is that, with respect to the total local population, the ratio of the lower middle and working classes in the latter is much narrower than in the former. (The same, of course, is the case with the SMC and the upper middle class, while plutocratic magnates and politicians are exclusively enfranchised in Córdoba and Fortin.) Moreover, many rural working-class people, especially factory workers and specialized craftsmen, gravitate to the hub where most of the factories and places of work are located.

Small Mestizo folk communities may have their own class structure, including local elites composed of the most affluent and influential local families, but in terms of regional stratification, whatever populations they may have, above subsistence peasants and the dispossessed, are either lower middle or working class. In other words, the transition from the lowest rungs of regional stratification is conditioned directly or indirectly by the city: either as a model to emulate locally or by (daily, weekly, or permanent) migration to the city to practice a craft that they may have traditionally learned in the community or elsewhere in search of better economic opportunities. The fortunate ones work in a shop or a factory, but the majority (housemaids, waitresses, gardeners, earning the minimum salary or less) increase the number of the urban dispossessed, as detailed in the following chapter.

Expressive Analysis

Lower-middle- and working-class families are also very much concerned with material acquisition, but unlike the SMC, expressive emulation is subordinated to the requirements of acquiring what they regard as constituting a proper standard of living: decent housing, necessary household appliances, adequate clothing, appropriate diet, and enough money for basic forms of entertainment. The sources of vicarious emulation are partly provided by the SMC families, with whom they interact in a subordinate social position, but mostly by what they read in newspapers and magazines, what they see on television, and some, particularly store and shop owners, in their occasional trips to Mexico City to buy merchandise and supplies. From a different perspective, upward mobility for most lower-middle- and working-class families is not a primary concern, nor is it determined primarily by expressive emulation but by the intrinsic desire to improve their economic lot. This attitude is perceived by the people as a right, as the country increasingly becomes more democratic and egalitarian. This is a rather recent phenomenon that has become widespread among the lower middle and working classes since the rule of the PRI came to an end in 2000. What has not happened is the realization that rights imply responsibilities, or, as an uneducated but aware working-class informant put it when President Vicente Fox won the election and the people were euphoric about how things would greatly change: "La gente tiene la ilusión de que porque ganó el PAN las cosas van a cambiar radicalmente. Los cambios vendrán cuando cambiemos nosotros mismos, y nos volvamos conscientes de nuestras obligaciones de ciudadanos" (People have the illusion that because the PAN won, things will radically change. Changes will come when we [the people] change and become more conscious of our obligations as citizens).[9]

It should be emphasized that, as a corollary of basic improvements in living standards, most lower-middle-class and working-class people are not consciously upwardly mobile. The notable exceptions are the most affluent small store and shop owners, many of whom not only identify with the SMC but also aspire to be their social equals. This comparatively small group, probably no more than three hundred families, assiduously emulates the SMC, as the latter expressively emulates the upper middle class. Moreover, the material domains and patterns of behavior are basically the same, except that the passage from lower middle class to the SMC is faster, as SMC families are less uppity and fastidious than upper-middle-class families, but fraught with many expressive faux pas, determined primarily by the lower degree of formal and social education of lower-middle-class people. Beyond satisfying basic necessities, upwardly mobile lower-middle-class families engage in expressive emulation in such domains as household decoration, personal behavior, and dress, to name the most sought after. In so doing, lower-middle-class families incur the scorn of the SMC as well as people of their own class. Their more educated children, however, serve as a moderating influence in guiding the process and form of upward mobility. This process is seen most strikingly when college-educated young people live with their parents; the embryonic class differences are often marked. Equipped with a different perspective on what constitutes a good life, and how to achieve it, the educated young invariably establish their own residences immediately after marriage and are launched, independently of their parents, on the way to an SMC existence. Parents do not begrudge their educated children's aspirations; on the contrary, they applaud them, for the aim of obtaining a college degree is to rise in the economic and social scales.[10]

The whitening syndrome among the upwardly mobile lower working class does take place but not as frequently as among the superordinately placed and the SMC. In the quest for SMC acceptance, parents tend to gravitate toward SMC families phenotypically similar to them, that is, to less criollo, more Mestizo phenotypes, thereby significantly diminishing the whitening syndrome. Not so their college-educated offspring. Much less constrained by racial proclivities and concerns, phenotypical appearance does not play an expressive role in the game of upward mobility. Rather, the aim of the educated young at this level of the regional stratification system is to generate the perception that they are as able to be good professionals or to do well in business as any SMC or upper-middle-class individual. This attitude often strikes most SMC and upper-middle-class people as uppity, and it constitutes one of the most glaring racist traits of the more phenotypically Caucasoid sectors of the population. But this new development, probably no more than fifteen years old, also indicates that the situation is changing and that education, or training, if you will, is making a difference in ameliorating some of the racist traits of Mexican society. I say this because I have observed the same phenomenon in several regions of central Mexico.

Are there any fundamental differences in the expressive behavior of the lower middle and working classes? The answer is no, but the loci and emphases of expression are somewhat different, which are essentially determined by the generally closer cultural and physical proximity of the working class to the folk situation. Again, I am referring to Córdoba-Fortin, the urban hub of the region. Specific domains of expression will clarify the matter.

Household decoration increases in expressive significance as people move up on the social scale. Concentrating on the main room of the house (not necessarily a living room), at the working-class level decoration plays an insignificant role. There is little beyond a few plastic adornments such as wall calendars, clocks, and family photographs, and, on the sparse furniture (a table, a breakfront-like contraption [*trastero*] to store dishes and cups, occasionally a trunk and a sofa-chair, and several store-bought metal chairs or homemade wooden chairs), trinkets such as seashell ashtrays and plaster religious figurines. (Among working-class families, the abode itself is a more important domain of expression than its decoration. If they reside in a house, they will plant a small garden, or decorate the outside of the house with potted plants and vines. If they live in an apartment, most likely, in a low-rent, government-sponsored project, they will do something to improve their cramped conditions.) The subtle, diagnostic transition to lower-middle-class status is marked by significant changes in decoration. The main room of the house becomes a living room, in the conventional (American) sense: furnished with store-bought pieces (sofas and matching chairs, upholstered chairs, a center table, and occasionally a breakfront). The walls may be decorated with posters, bucolic paintings on velvet,[11] and tanned pelts of wild animals. The passage to SMC status is marked by reaching another notch in household decoration: the living room furniture is more elegant, there is concern with matching the colors of furniture and curtains (which are absent from lower-middle-class houses, the windows of which may occasionally have *visillos,* or crude shades), and the walls may be decorated with oil paintings and watercolors by local artists. It would take an entire chapter to describe the household decoration, but I think I have made the point: household decoration is the most diagnostic trait of class membership in the middle stratum of regional society.

There are a few differences in religious expression between lower-middle-class and working-class people, most noticeably in the physical manifestations of Catholicism. For example, being on the whole closer to the folk situation, working-class families preserve the folk form and decoration of the household "altar" to the saints of their devotion, whereas lower-middle-class families, most of them more than a generation from their folk origins, do not. The practice of rites and ceremonies is centered for lower-middle-class families almost exclusively in church, whereas among working-class families, many are still practiced in the privacy of the household. But the beliefs, ideology, and teleology of lower-middle-class and working-class Catholics are the same. The cult of the saints is basically unchanged, and the traditional religious covenant binding individuals and the deity functions the same as in the folk context, except that it no longer has a collective component.

The expressive realization of compadrazgo and kinship and the celebration of the rites and ceremonies of the life and annual cycles is the same in lower-middle-class and working-class families, and again quite close to the folk situation. They evoke the highly ritualized nature of personal interaction in these aspects of social and religious life, which urban living has modernized but not entirely secularized. The model of behavior of lower-middle- and working-class urbanites, most of them less than three generations from their folk roots, retain an expressive component that remains basically constant until individuals and families make the transition to an SMC existence. Compadrazgo, kinship, and the realization of the life and ritual cycles cease then to be "sacred" institutions and become regulated by economic considerations, orthodox religion, and other constraints. At least in this limited sociocultural domain, there is a kind of unbroken expressive continuity from rural-folk to urban, lower-middle-class existence.

Dress, personal demeanor, and verbal behavior are domains of expression that are noticeable indicators of upward mobility. The transition from a rural-folk to an urban working-class environment is the most marked. It should be noted, however, that this change is also experienced in rural communities, but there it is invariably an individual process, never entailing class-mobility consequences. This is engendered in the urban context by better and more focused economic and educational opportunities that inevitably lead to a change in dress style, social and physical conduct, and patterns of speech. College-educated offspring of lower-middle-class families, and occasionally of working-class families, play a significant role in this expressive transformation, to the extent that they are instrumental in influencing their parents' dress, behavior, and speech. This is a self-serving and welcome attitude that is part of the dual existence that the upwardly mobile, educated young lead vis-à-vis their parents. But it is also a significant mechanism in the process of upward mobility of lower-middle-class families, which generates new forms of expressive behavior. Thus expressive emulation of the SMC and upward mobility are two sides of the same process that is effectively transforming the middle stratum of regional society.

Finally, returning to the whitening syndrome, unlike the SMC context, the generated expressive behavior is not so much an aspect of upward mobility (i.e., a component of expressive emulation) as a manifestation of deep-seated themes of Mexican social behavior everywhere that intrinsically favor Caucasoid-looking individuals. This spawns a wide range of expressive behavior, from perceiving as intrinsically more beautiful (and favoring) infants and children with Caucasoid features to searching for spouses for the same reason. Suffice it to say that I have given enough examples of this pervasive and unfortunate syndrome. The noxiousness of this syndrome has been incalculable, and the racism that it engenders has significantly prevented the formation of a more egalitarian and just society.

Chapter 5 | ＴHE DISPOSSESSED

Rural Lumpen, Subsistence Peasants,
and the Indian-Mestizo Dichotomy

*S*o far I have centered the description and analysis in
the context of the city, primarily the Córdoba-Fortin
urban hub. Here I am concerned with the rural context and its relationship to the urban hub. Specifically, this chapter addresses the following
topics: (1) the local class structure of rural Mestizo communities and the
differences with respect to the lower middle and working classes in the urban environment; (2) internal social mobility and the mobility that obtains
in permanent migration to the city and in the context of community-
centered migration; (3) interethnic relations, the formation of mixed communities, and the configuration of *mestizaje* (racial mixing) since the 1910
Revolution; (4) the interrelationship of class, race, and ethnicity in the
contemporary changing context of the short-range historical perspective
(1950 – 2000); (5) the passage from Indian to Mestizo status and the social
and economic variables that generated it (1850 – 1950); (6) implications of
the regional Indian-Mestizo dichotomy, how it is manifested in incipient
class formation, and the factors that have been instrumental in its perpetuation; (7) the nature and configuration of the Indian "persona" and how
it has influenced the formation of the rural and urban lower middle and
working classes.

THE RURAL ENVIRONMENT: SIZE OF COMMUNITIES,
DEMOGRAPHIC COMPOSITION, ECONOMIC ORGANIZATION

There are approximately two hundred rural communities in the twenty-
seven municipios that I have included in the Córdoba region. They range
from small hamlets (*rancherías* and *congregaciones*) with populations of
100 to 600 people to large full-fledged villages with populations of 1,500
to 8,000. As I indicated in Chapter 2, the dominant settlement pattern is

the nucleated village, with a few seminucleated and dispersed villages, Indian as well as Mestizo. Some examples put matters in perspective.

The municipio of Tequila has a population of about 6,000. The *cabecera* (head town) is a nucleated community of more than 1,200 inhabitants; the remaining population is dispersed in isolated homesteads or groups of four of five households built close together (no more than 20 or 30 yards apart). The homesteads and clusters usually are located from 300 to 800 yards apart. The population of the cabecera is composed almost entirely of Mestizos who are from the municipio or settled there from from Córdoba or Orizaba for business reasons. The Indian population is among the most traditional in the region: about 30 percent are still monolingual in Nahuatl, and most men and women still wear traditional dress. The economy of the municipio, beyond meager agricultural subsistence, is centered in the cabecera; Mestizo families own all the general stores and small specialty stores and control the local market (*tianguis*), which takes place every Sunday. The overwhelming majority of the Indian population ekes out a subsistence living, barely above starvation, by cultivating crops, primarily corn and beans, on the steep slopes of mountains and hills, minimally supplemented by weaving a few woolen items such as shawls, bags, and sashes, which are sold in Tequila and nearby cities and towns. During the past twenty years, there has been some community-centered labor migration to regional urban centers, but it has not yet become generalized. Labor migrants, almost always men, occupy the lowest rung of the gainfully employed, most of them earning less than the minimum salary.

The municipio of Ixtazoquitlan is composed of the cabecera, whose population is about 8,000 people, and five satellite hamlets and villages, whose populations range from 300 to 900, for a total population of about 10,000.[1] All inhabitants of the municipio have a mixed economy of subsistence agriculture (mostly corn, beans, and some fruit trees, mostly criollo, or domestic, apples and pears) and cash cropping (sugarcane, chayotes, and some coffee). The ethnicity of the population is a mixture of Mestizos, one or two generations removed from the Indian past, and a rather large Indian-transitional population (perhaps as high as 30 percent of the total population of the municipio), living in close proximity in the cabecera as well as satellite communities. Most of the people who have achieved lower-middle-class status are concentrated in the cabecera. They constitute no more than 10 percent of the population; these individuals and families are the owners of all commercial establishments — *tortillerías* (tortilla shops), *cantinas* (bars), *changarros* (very small shops), small general stores, and other small businesses—in the small towns and large villages in the region. Labor migration daily (to Córdoba, Orizaba, Fortin) and weekly (to as far away as Puebla and Veracruz) has been an important aspect of the local economy since the late 1950s. Approximately 35 percent of the families have members working outside the municipio. The labor migrants constitute the local working class. More than half of the population are subsistence or cash cropping peasants, including Mestizos and Indians from all settlements in the municipio.

Naranjal has a rather homogeneous Mestizo population of 5,500. About 1,500 are concentrated in the cabecera and the rest in seven hamlets. All are nucleated settlements close to one another and clustered around the cabecera, so that the municipio looks like an extended settlement. As far as I was able to establish, Naranjal became a Mestizo community about thirty years ago. When I conducted the first survey of the region (Nutini 2004), there were a few Nahuatl speakers. Today there are no Nahuatl speakers, Indian dress has completely disappeared, and many Indian customs and usages have been modified. I am unable to explain why Naranjal became a Mestizo community while adjacent communities remained Indian.[2] Until twenty-five years ago Naranjal was an important center of citrus cultivation. Since then its orange groves have greatly deteriorated, and this aspect of the local economy is no longer important. Rather, the local economy, like most adjacent municipios, is a combination of subsistence agriculture, cash cropping, and labor migration.[3] Unlike most municipios that are one or two generations removed from a significant Indian component, labor migration from Naranjal involves a large number of women, which is probably the result of the greater Mestizoization of this municipio.

With slight variations, these are the basic patterns of ethnic, demographic, and economic organization of communities and municipios in the hilly and mountainous areas above Córdoba. They are all located in tierra templada and tierra fría. The main differences concern the Indian-Mestizo composition and the local economy, that is, the mixture of subsistence and cash crops (which varies with altitude) and the degree of labor migration. By contrast, all municipios below Córdoba are located in tierra caliente, are more homogeneous, and are different ethnically, demographically, and economically. First, with two notable exceptions, Amatlán de los Reyes and El Otate, there are no Indian municipios or communities with a significant Indian presence. (At the time of the 1910 Revolution, there was a rather large Nahuatl-speaking population in this part of the region. Since then it has largely disappeared, some of them since 1970, when I conducted my first survey of the area. And today, these communities are in the last stages of transition to Mestizo status.) The ethnic composition of the area is largely Mestizo but with a significant Negroid component. (As I indicated in Chapter 2, there are no black communities, but individual black and mulatto phenotypes are common everywhere.) Second, the people of the tierra caliente are economically better off than those of the tierra templada and the tierra fría; there is more arable land, and the quality of the soil is better. This relative agricultural affluence has two main consequences: there is less outward labor migration; and the local (communal) commercial establishment is more extensive. Another consequence is that cash cropping (sugarcane, bananas, avocados, mangoes, and citrus) is by far more important than the subsistence cultivation of staple crops. Third, the settlement pattern is entirely nucleated, and the communities are much more compact than those at higher elevations. The municipios are larger and more populated and present an outward aspect of reasonable prosperity. Fourth, communities and municipios of the tierra caliente are more integrated into the national, urban culture.

This description places the region in comparative perspective for the analysis of rural stratification and mobility. The analysis focuses primarily on municipal head towns and large villages, as in most cases hamlets are essentially part of them.

THE LOWER MIDDLE AND WORKING CLASSES, THE DISPOSSESSED, AND THEIR RELATIONSHIP TO THE CITY

The rural lower middle and working classes can only be understood as an extension of the urban, national class structure, as I have made clear in Chapter 4. Not only is their existence predicated on an urban model, but their economic realization is an extension of industrialization and the economic growth and diversification that accompanies it. It is tempting to talk about local replicas of the social stratification of the urban hub of Córdoba-Fortin. This would be spurious and a distortion of the economic reality of the region. Class distinctions do exist but are contingent on exogenous factors such as labor migration and the cultural influence of the city, tempered by the basically egalitarian configuration of a peasant society.

Structurally and expressively, there is no solid middle class in rural communities, and local elites are the owners of the small shops and stores invariably found in cabeceras and the larger settlements and occasionally even in hamlets. This local lower-middle-class elite also includes a few small farmers (individuals and families who may own properties of 10 hectares or more), and owners of trucks for transportation, and other small business enterprises. This elite is very small, probably not larger than 6 percent of the families of the average rural community. A notch below are the daily and weekly labor migrants to factories and the many businesses to the nearby cities and to other large urban centers within a radius of 250 miles. (Seasonal migration to the United States has been a significant aspect of the regional economy since the mid-1950s. This has been one of the sources of the growth of the rural lower middle class, for with the money saved, they were able to return to their communities and set up businesses. Labor migrants to the United States generally were adults who always came back. This has changed in the past decade. Labor migrants are now mostly young, and many do not return; when they do return, they do not have much to show, as whatever they earned they spent in the United States.) The wages of well-established daily and weekly labor migrants may be three to seven times the minimum salary. This category of labor migrants, however, does not constitute more than 25 percent of the total daily and weekly migrant labor force and consists exclusively of young and adult men.

At the bottom are the dispossessed, which includes the minimally gainfully employed (making the minimum salary, often less) and the Indian and Mestizo subsistence peasants who cultivate one hectare or less per family. Subsistence peasants must periodically hire themselves out as day laborers to farmers and the more prosperous members of the community, who, nevertheless, cannot afford to pay the minimum salary. The minimally employed, both men and women, constitute about 60 percent of the labor force and are engaged almost exclusively in daily migration, except for housemaids who usually visit their communities biweekly. The most common occupations are housemaids, waitresses, waiters, gardeners, and street sweepers in the regional cities. Daily labor migration is facilitated by a passable system of roads and a good system of transportation. Under these conditions, labor migrants of both kinds are never more than an hour and a half by motorized transportation from their communities.

The rural lower middle and working classes are in most ways, at least outwardly, an extension of the urban centers: their material culture is basically the same, their economies are intimately interrelated, and it would be hard to pinpoint significant differences in the social and religious realization of the events of the life and annual cycles. Physical isolation and lack of social communication have been the main factors that kept communities traditional, particularly the municipios of the tierra templada and the tierra fría. For example, most of the communities to the west and southwest of Córdoba in 1910 were Indian-traditional and Indian-transitional. Today, most are Mestizo-transitional and Mestizo-secularized communities. This change may be attributed first to the construction of roads, then to the establishment of motorized transportation, and finally to the diffusion of the means of communication, radio and then television. The combined effect of these variables does not explain the survival of the few Indian communities, since they too were similarly affected. This likelihood was suggested to me by the fact that Indian communities today only minimally engage in daily or weekly migration, and when they do migrate in numbers, individuals or entire families settle permanently beyond the confines of the region. Moreover, as I discuss below, there are several aspects in the structural and expressive configuration of Indian communities that make them resistant to transition to Mestizo status.

The rural lower middle and working classes may be regarded as cultural brokers bridging the city and the country as a kind of homogenizing mechanism. Commuting from their communities to their places of work and spending a great deal of time in urban and industrial environments, working-class people are important agents shaping the sociocultural milieus of their communities, that is, as instruments that created, and continue to create, a worldview that is steadily departing from its Indian roots (this theme is explored more fully below). Similarly, the lower middle class, composed of small merchants, store owners, and farmers, is, by the nature of its members' activities, intimately and continually tied to the city, but the effect on the changing rural environment is in different domains. At the start of the rapid process of change more than two generations ago, their mercantile and economic activities were the main factors that brought the city closer to the community: they introduced new household wares, foodstuffs, consumption patterns, and so on. Now, and during the past twenty years, with the greater physical mobility of rural peoples of all ethnic backgrounds, this faction of local store and shop owners has almost disappeared. However, as owners of the commerce that goes on in rural communities, their economic importance is still significant: they sell on credit to the poorest peasants (those who would seldom venture beyond the confines of their municipios or are not able to buy on credit in the cities), they serve as outlets in Indian-Mestizo municipios for the articles produced by Indian craftsmen, and they serve as middlemen for providing the community with fertilizer and agricultural implements. More important sociologically, the lower middle class serves as the sector to emulate in the process of upward mobility: their economic success is the main attraction, but perhaps more significantly, lower-middle-class families are perceived as the local model for a better way of life that the average subsistence peasant family can realistically aspire to achieve.

Many dispossessed migrant laborers, after seven or more years, settle permanently in the city and join the ranks of the urban dispossessed. This obtains primarily in the Córdoba-Fortín hub. The more upwardly mobile of this lumpen workforce, by dint of hard work and perseverance, make their way into white-collar jobs. (Very few dispossessed become working-class factory workers; I have no explanation for this phenomenon.) The most enterprising obtain a high school or technical education by going to night school and taking advantage of adult educational opportunities provided by the state and federal governments. It is not unusual, for example, for a street sweeper or a housemaid to obtain a high school or technical education after ten or twelve years in this city, and this education provides a means to a white-collar existence.[4] It was impossible to estimate the degree of upward mobility of the dispossessed who had been born in rural communities. But I was able to establish with certainty that after a decade or so, there are few if any structural and expressive differences between dispossessed families of rural and urban provenance. Although the former may occasionally visit their rural communities of origin, they are both an undifferentiated part of the same lumpen. Thus in this chapter I describe and analyze together the dispossessed in the city and in the country, pointing out any differences of structural and expressive realization in these two milieus. Before I do so, it is necessary to describe the lower middle and working classes as the rural "elites" vis-à-vis which the dispossessed must be placed.

The Rural Lower Middle and Working Classes

As I have suggested, the urban and rural lower middle and working classes are part of the same continuum and have essentially the same configuration. There are differences, but they are mainly explained by the greater cultural complexity and diversification of the urban environment. In Chapter 4, I described the lower middle and working classes; here I confine my discussion to the differences, why they exist, and their implications.

Except that the lower middle class, as the rural elite and the owners of all local businesses, have more influence and prestige than the working class, the same relationship between them obtains as in urban environments. To some extent, the position of the rural lower middle class in urban communities is like that of the SMC in urban communities; without stretching the point, its economic influence has functions similar to the mercantile, but not professional, SMC in the city. This structural fact underlies the most salient differences between the rural and urban middle classes, which significantly enhances the local expressive significance of the former.

The rural lower middle class is significantly smaller than that in urban settings. This is because the proliferation of stores and shops is much greater in the city. The working class is also proportionally smaller, because the rural population is also smaller than the combined population of the five cities of the region. This means that, in absolute terms, more working-class people are permanently enfranchised in the cities than are migrants from rural communities.[5] This generalization applies mostly to municipios in the tierra templa and tierra fría, where the working class of migrant laborers is proportionally higher than in the tierra caliente, where there is more arable land and the quality of the soil is better. In fact, there is a noticeable difference in economic affluence between these two parts of the region at the communal level.

The composition of the lower middle class is considerably less complex than in the cities. In addition to the elite, described above, primary and secondary school teachers and nurses in local clinics complete the list. To the extent that there are no professionals (e.g., physicians, lawyers, engineers) enfranchised in rural communities, there is no supporting personnel (e.g., secretaries, receptionists, technicians). Insofar as there are lower-middle-class personnel in this category living in rural communities, they are part of the labor migrant force who have white-collar jobs in the city.

Given the simplified nature of the lower middle and working classes in the rural environment, the urban distinctions between salaried workers and the self-employed and between white-collar and blue-collar workers also obtain but in a more attenuated form due to the more egalitarian nature of a folk society, in some cases only one generation removed from the Indian past. The former is minimally realized but latently present. The latter is specifically realized in parents guiding their children to aim for white-collar occupations and helping them financially to achieve these ends. Indeed, vicariousness is an important component of this syndrome and is realized to a significant degree.

Ethnically, the urban and rural lower middle and working classes are essentially the same, except that people in the tierra templada and tierra fría exhibit a greater degree of phenotypical Indian traits, whereas people in the tierra caliente exhibit more phenotypically Negroid features. The ethnic-phenotypic population of the Córdoba region may be summarized as follows. In the hub, one finds the greatest phenotypic variation. The only population that is not adequately represented are Indians. Almost the entire Caucasoid population is enfranchised in the hub, although the other four cities of the region have small nuclei of Caucasoids. Moreover, the hub also congregates more than 60 percent of the criollo, light Mestizo population. The population of the rural communities in the tierra templada and the tierra fría is composed largely of dark Mestizo phenotypes with about 20 percent of mulatto phenotypes. The population of rural communities in the tierra caliente is composed primarily of markedly Negroid phenotypes, with about 40 percent of Mestizo phenotypes. Nahuatl Indian communities, with the exceptions noted above, are found mostly in the municipios of the tierra templada and tierra fría.

The whitening syndrome in rural communities, as far as it is an aspect of socioeconomic mobility, is practically nonexistent, but it has another dimension in the life of the people. Essentially, this is the deeply ingrained tendency to favor lighter, more Caucasoid-looking infants and children among one's progeny and, in general, the attitude that people are more beautiful and acceptable, the more they exhibit European features. Particularly in the case of children, this kind of favoritism can be devastating, and I have observed that it increases as people rise on the social scale.[6]

There are no objectifiable differences between rural and urban lower-middle- and working-class families. The perception exists, however, that the former are more affluent, and, at least concerning the working class, the reason adduced is that they also have some land that they cultivate, which increases the disposable income of the family. Whether this is true or not I was not able to determine; the real differences are expressive, as I discuss below.

In rural communities, the lower middle class, by virtue of its elite position, has on the whole a better standard of living than the migratory working class. Their residences are more elaborate in terms of furniture and appliances and in every way are as well appointed as those of their urban counterparts. The economy of the rural elites is quite standardized, and even the richest have lifestyles similar to the least affluent; it is as though, by design, they do not want to flaunt their wealth.[7] In contrast, among the migratory working class, there is much more variation in economic affluence and the lifestyle that goes with it, which I discuss in my expressive analysis.

It is in the domains of kinship and religion that the rural lower middle and working classes and the dispossessed differ the most from their urban counterparts. Let us take kinship first. Family and household organization is more tightly organized and has some well-defined corporate functions. The nonresidential extended family, or patrilineal minimal lineage as Robichaux (1996) terms it, is the most important kinship unit beyond the household. It is a comparatively large group, occasionally composed of as many as six or seven patrilaterally related households, and has significant corporate functions of a social, religious, and economic nature. The compadrazgo system is the most complex and extensive in the region, including the Mestizo and Indian dispossessed. In some communities, it has as many as twenty-one practicing types, which approaches the complexity and extension of the institution in rural Tlaxcala.

Rural people practice a syncretic type of Catholicism that departs significantly from the more orthodox Catholicism of urban environments, which is basically the same as that I have described for the Tlaxcala-Pueblan Valley (Nutini 1988). This folk Catholicism is markedly different from the national Catholic religion of Mexico, and it is characterized by three main attributes. First, it is more monolatrous than it is monotheistic; essentially, no categorical distinction operationally obtains between God and the saints (including all advocations of the Virgin Mary). In theological terms, this means the confusion of *latria* and *dulia*. Second, it has an annual cycle of rites and ceremonies centered on a cargo system of positions elected or nominated by the community. This system is posited on a conception of religion that postulates a covenant between the individual and the community and the deities (both Christian and folk). The former, to avail themselves of the protection and good offices of the latter, must perform an extensive, and costly, complex of rites and ceremonies; failing to do so detracts from individual happiness and the proper conditions for a harmonious communal existence. Once individuals and the community have complied with their part of the bargain, everything else is unimportant or takes second place. Third, this is fundamentally a pragmatic religion, surprisingly devoid of moral and ethical components. Ethics and morality are regulated by the social structure in operation. This is the legacy of pre-Hispanic polytheism: the nearly five centuries of Catholicism that permeate Mexican folk religion do not entirely disappear in the transition to the city.

What happens to folk religion in the context of change, secularization, and upward social mobility? Essentially, what I have called "Christianization," that is, the increased importance of Christian ethics in the conduct of everyday life and, conversely, the disappearance of the regulations and constraints of the social structure in operation as the locus of morality and social control.[8] The process of Christianization begins in the rural context, particularly in the largest communities and municipal cabeceras, which are the most secularized and have the most contact with the outside, but it acquires its most orthodox expression in the city. However, it should be noted that strict Catholic morality is very unlikely to replace completely the strong hold that the social structure in action has on the people. Research conducted in the city of Puebla and Mexico City reveals that lower-class people, with two or three generations of urban residence, function in a moral no-man's land somewhere between traditional social ethics and orthodox Catholic ethics. Indeed, this is the moral environment in which the working class, the dispossessed, and to some extent the lower-middle class function in the Córdoba-Fortin hub.

Evangelism in the rural areas is as strong as in urban environments, but there are some significant differences. There are a few native evangelist congregations, mainly of La Luz del Mundo (the Light of the World), but they have not been as successful as evangelical Protestant sects. The most successful are Jehovah's Witnesses and Pentecostals; less so, Seventh-Day Adventists, and Mormons are just beginning to make converts. The congregations, which in the cities may be as large as 500 or 600, in rural communities are seldom more than about 150. Finally, the Indians so far have resisted conversion, and only in Ixhuatlancillo is there a small Jehovah's Witness congregation. The relationship between Catholics and evangelists has so far been tense; there are occasional confrontations, but it has not yet degenerated into serious violence. This is much more likely to occur in rural communities than in the cities, and, in my estimation, it is just a matter of time.

One cannot collectively speak of class consciousness among the rural lower middle and working class. Individuals may occasionally express views that may be interpreted as class based, but the concept of class membership that encompasses and denotes occupation, economic activity, or social position is weak. Local lower-middle-class elite individuals are the most conscious of occupying a specific niche in the structure of the community, not unlike that of the urban SMC. And insofar as the local working-class exhibits class consciousness, it is as a function of being part of the urban working class.[9] What is lacking in the rural lower middle and working classes is mechanisms of collective action, elements that are invariably aspects of kinship and community, which largely disappear in the transition to the urban context.

Expressive Analysis

Given the adequacy of the road system, good transportation, and accessibility to all forms of communication during the past generation, the country has been brought increasingly closer to the city. Except for the hold of folk kinship and religion, the rural lower middle and working classes are essentially the same as their urban counterparts, as I noted above. Under such conditions, the expressive aspects of these classes differ mostly as determined by the facts of demography.[10] Again, I will quickly describe the most significant differences in patterns of expression vis-à-vis the urban environment.

The expressive array of the rural lower middle and working classes is also centered on material culture, the household, and the acquisition of goods as a means to demonstrate that, though they identify themselves as folk people, they do not consider themselves "culturally" inferior to city folk of the same status. (This is especially true of the prominent local economic elites.) The best way to encapsulate this local worldview is as a case of collective keeping up with the urban Joneses, that is, to demonstrate that they have kept up with the latest amenities that the commercial world of the cities can offer. Thus their homes are as well appointed as their urban counterparts' homes: passable furniture, good refrigerators, kitchen stoves, televisions, record players, and other appliances. It is not unusual to find local lower-middle-class households that are better appointed than those of their affluent urban counterparts. Although elite families may own cars, their expressive ideal is to own a good pickup truck, the latest model if possible. Having no immediate model, the main source of expressive emulation is television, and they occasionally learn of new trends during trips outside the region on business.

The migrant working class exhibits similar proclivities, but being less affluent than the local elites, they are not as consumed with collectively keeping up with the Joneses. Moreover, the loci of expression are slightly different. The household is an important domain, but working-class migrants channel their resources more pragmatically into the educational and economic well-being of their offspring, quite often forgoing the purchase of an old car and other amenities they could afford. From this standpoint, expressive realization is intimately tied to upward mobility, for they instill in their children that education is the key to a better life but not necessarily in the community. This attitude means also that there is more permanent outward migration by the children of the working class than by the children of the local economic elite, as the latter encourage their children to stay home and take care of their established businesses. Because they spend a good deal of time in the city in contact with different social and economic milieus, quite often local working-class people are more innovative in their overall expressive array than are local elites.

The offspring of local lower-middle- and working-class families with a technical and, occasionally, college education (mainly in primary and secondary education and business administration) quite often function as expressive brokers. They are conscious of their folk roots but quite intent on demonstrating to all and sundry that they have come up in the world. From this standpoint, rural, educated, young men and women are the most upwardly mobile in the community. Closely related to this aspect of mobility is the realization of the whitening syndrome, in essentially the same way that I described it among the urban lower middle and working classes. However, the syndrome is much less accentuated among the educated young and practically nonexistent among those who have permanently made the transition to city. It should be noted, however, that the whitening syndrome is always latent and surfaces in the most unsuspected places along the entire range of the stratification system. This is testimony to centuries of colonial domination that will be difficult to entirely uproot.

The above description exhausts the differences between the urban and rural environments. Moreover, the expressive array of the rural lower middle class and the migratory working class entails fewer differences than that of these classes in the urban environment. Finally, let me address the two major domains of expression that characterize and significantly distinguish these two social classes from their urban equivalents, namely, the folk-traditional and the urban-secularized milieus of kinship and religious expressive realization.

Kinship and compadrazgo are important domains of expressive realization. The loci of the former are the extended family (which has a rather high degree of incidence in rural communities of the Córdoba region; in some communities, at any given time, as many as 40 percent of the people are living in extended family arrangements) and the nonresidential extended family, the only functional, effective unit beyond the household. Kinship behavior is highly ritualized, accompanies most events of the annual and life cycles, and has many expressive manifestations. A few examples demonstrate the diversity of kinship and compadrazgo expression.[11]

Of all kinship institutions, marriage is inherently the most determinant source for the realization of expression. This is certainly the case in most sectors of Mexican society, particularly in Indian and Mestizo folk society. The baroque elaboration of the wedding ceremony in the rural communities of the Córdoba region may be the most complex that I have observed in central Mexico; only the Tlaxcala-Pueblan Valley surpasses it. The expressive rites and specific behavior that accompany the main events of the wedding (the banquets in the house of the groom, bride, and groom's baptismal padrino; the long series of orations that attend the handing over of the bride to the family of the groom and the reception of the bride in the groom's household; the counsel and admonition to the couple by the kinsmen of the bride and groom in the house of the groom's baptismal padrino; etc.) are designed to establish and specify the new status of the bride, the proper behavior of bride and groom toward one another and toward their respective in-laws, and the rights and obligations of both sets of kinsmen. Equally significant, contracting a proper alliance spawns many specific domains of expression, including patterns of courtship, searching for the appropriate marriage partner, and generating goodwill with one's in-laws. The exogenous aspects of marriage, primarily the wedding, are also significant; it is the event in the life cycle that attracts the most kinsmen permanently living in the city or engaged in seasonal migration throughout Mexico and in the United States. Marriage, then, is an event that brings kinsmen together to renew ties that have been dormant or to intensify others that are socially and economically beneficial for those who have gone away and those who remain in the community. Thus the marriage domain of expression may be regarded as a mechanism for preserving kinship identity and integrity in the context of intense labor migration.

Remembering illustrious ancestors who served the kin group well or did some outstanding service for the social and religious welfare of the community is also important. This is done primarily during "homecoming," which for the communities of the Córdoba region is the period from Christmas to Epiphany (December 16 to January 6), when families that have settled elsewhere and labor migrants who have been away for a long time visit the community for a few days.[12] Homecoming is what I have called elsewhere (Nutini 1988, 397–400) a period of "sacred intensification," when those who have gone away return to be with their kinsmen, neighbors, and friends. It is a highly ritualistic and symbolic occasion when old ties are renewed and intensified and the country and the city are brought together in a single world of existence. During homecoming, everybody is on their best behavior, characterized by restraint, circumspection, and accommodation. The people avoid situations that may lead to friction or confrontation, presents are exchanged, there is a great deal of visiting, and there is no indulgence in excessive drinking. An important aspect of this complex is the offering of banquets or masses by kin groups and the community to individuals (distinguished past cargo holders and civil officials) who have performed exceptional service to the community. In sum, sacralized homecomings are periods of almost continuous ritual and ceremonial activity, the main function of which is to maintain city-country connections, thus prolonging the folk roots of those no longer enfranchised in the community and facilitating labor migration, by now an adaptive way of life without which the community could not survive economically.[13] Although this complex has key structural consequences for the adaptive survival of the community, the context in which it is discharged is expressive in the purest form.

Even more than kinship, ritual kinship, or compadrazgo, is a manifold domain where expression is realized in manifold forms. Lacking the "natural," blood-determined injunctions and constraints of kinship, compadrazgo, as a sacred institution (which is egalitarian-horizontal, structurally symmetrical, containing prescriptive and optional types), is largely configured and regulated by expressive variables and behavior. This means that, in the absence of rules of behavior and mechanisms of control (characteristics of all kinship systems), expressive considerations in specific contexts generate the ideological guidelines for the structural discharge of compadrazgo types. The ensemble of each of the twenty-one types that I have recorded for the region entails its own expressive injunctions and constraints, which results in specific structural discharge. It is beyond the scope of this description to detail how compadrazgo is structured and what its functions are, but a few generalizations may put matters in perspective.

Compadrazgo types are ranked as sacramental (having to do with the sacraments of the church) and nonsacramental (sanctifying events and occasions of a religious, social, and economic nature). In turn, the types of these subdivisions are ranked according to symbolic, social, and economic importance. Each of the sacramental and nonsacramental types is an expressive domain in its own right, but the entire compadrazgo system (i.e., the approximately fifteen types that are practiced in the average community) constitutes a major expressive domain of the total array of the community. People would rather slight the expressive behavior of kinship than that of compadrazgo, for in the contexts of physical and social mobility, the latter plays a more determinant role. The traditional flexibility and adaptability of compadrazgo is better suited to building the ties needed for a successful transition to the city and the support for making the necessary adjustments that urban living requires. Thus the profusion of expressive forms of behavior (the exaggerated ritualism, the elaborate speech, the contrived physical posture) that characterizes interaction among ritual kinsmen (which to the untrained eye may look spurious and somewhat risible) is the lubricant that makes compadrazgo an efficient institution in building networks and relationships.

Finally, religion is the most natural domain in which expression is intensely realized, though it is not as significant as compadrazgo and kinship for physical and social mobility. Centered on the cult of the saints and its accompanying *mayordomía* (religious sponsorship) system, local religion is an extended domain of expression. The twenty-odd mayordomías that constitute the cargo system in the average cabecera and communities of more than fifteen hundred people (which generally have satellite hamlets) are a year-round series of events that allow villagers to exercise their expressive talents and imaginations. The cargo system, of course, is structurally realized and has definite functions. Although manifestly the cargo system, and the mayordomías it entails, serves as a mechanism for local upward mobility, latently its discharge is the main mechanism generating goodwill with the supernatural, the human part of the covenant with the deity. In the transition to urban environments, folk religion is secularized and becomes Christianized, and these traditional functions disappear, thereby ceasing to have any significance for class formation and mobility.

The Rural Mestizo Dispossessed

There is no equivalent in the American class system for what I have called the urban and rural dispossessed. I use the term to denote not only what putatively may be called the lower lower class but also the poorest and most numerous sector of the population, living at a strictly subsistence level; the dispossessed are not starving, but they must constantly struggle to make ends meet. Even the Indians are better off economically than in all regions of refuge (as defined by Aguirre Beltrán 1967) with which I am acquainted (the Sierra de Puebla, the Mezquital, the Sierra de Guerrero, the Valle Nacional, and the Isthmus of Tehuantepec). In fact, the Córdoba region is one of the more prosperous in central and southern Mexico.

The rural dispossessed do not constitute a homogeneous group. The main cleavage is between Indian and Mestizo, the latter including individuals (in rural and urban environments) and communities in transition, that is, a generation or less from their Indian past. To define or demarcate an Indian community is not an easy task, nor is this the place to do it, but it hinges essentially on loss of native language and dress, forms of kinship and marriage, pagan elements in the syncretic folk religion, and the production of certain crafts as part of subsistence. Of course, it is easier to determine the transition of an individual than to do so when a *community* is no longer Indian. This is a relative matter, and no anthropologist yet has given a satisfactory answer to this vexing question.

There are, of course, a small number of urban-bred dispossessed who migrated to the city two or more generations ago and became disconnected from their rural communities of origin. These are the lumpen who never made it into the industrial or service working class or the lower middle class of small businessmen. (This is part of the tremendous growth of urbanization that not only Córdoba but also most cities in central Mexico have experienced for the past three generations; permanent migration to the city is the single most important variable in explaining this phenomenon.) The regional dispossessed are either enfranchised in rural communities or urban dwellers who did not become upwardly mobile because of lack of economic opportunities. Thus the urban dispossessed are not a separate category in the regional class system; they are part of the same rural-urban continuum. There are, of course, cultural differences between these two kinds of dispossessed. But first let me position the dispossessed with respect to the rural lower middle and working classes.

To a large extent, the Mestizo dispossessed share the same cultural tradition with the rural lower middle and working classes. There are some differences, however, that depend on individual and collective distance from the Indian past. This generalization pertains mainly to the municipios of tierra templada and tierra fría, parts of the region with formerly large Indian populations. Does the same obtain in tierra caliente, where the Indian population has been largely absent for at least one hundred years but where there is still a strong black "ethnic-phenotypic" component? The answer is a tentative no, for I do not know ethnographically that part of the region as well as the higher part, that is, above an elevation of 800 meters. I intuit, however, that in many communities of the tierra caliente some significant elements of black African culture may have survived, primarily in the ideological domain of witchcraft, sorcery, and curing. The last ethnically black community in the Córdoba region, as described by Aguirre Beltrán (1940), disappeared before the turn of the twentieth century.[14]

The great majority of rural Mestizo communities today are secularized. There are also a handful of communities that are Indian-transitional (i.e., traditional dress has disappeared, Nahuatl is spoken only by people over the age of fifty, and men minimally engage in labor migration within the region) and transitional-Mestizo (i.e., Nahuatl has essentially disappeared but may still be spoken by a few old people, and both men and women engage in labor migration). The situation is of course more complicated when one takes into consideration mixed communities, in which the passage from Indian to Mestizo status is underlain by individual considerations, often in the context of labor migration. There are cultural differences among these three types of rural Mestizo dispossessed, but they are not significant in the context of regional social mobility.

The situation in the Córdoba region has changed greatly since summer 1969, when Jean F. Nutini and I surveyed the region. By 2000, many Indian-transitional and transitional-Mestizo communities had made the transition to Mestizo-secularized status, almost all of them in the tierra templada and the tierra fría. The tierra caliente, on the other hand, had experienced this transformation more than a generation earlier, as intensive cash cropping (sugarcane, coffee, fruticulture) accelerated the change. Secularization, as far as I have been able to reconstruct it, began in the tierra caliente as early as the late 1930s. By the time of our survey, most of the communities were secularized, and today they adhere rather closely to the general pattern of the rural-urban continuum described above (a regional version of the urban-national culture of central Mexico). I predict that the same will obtain in the tierra templada and the tierra fría within the next two generation; that is, all Indian-transitional and transitional-Mestizo communities will become secularized. The big imponderable is, what will happen to the remaining Indian communities? Will they be able to resist the strong forces of modernization and secularization? I shall try to provide some answers to these questions below.

Before describing the cultural context of the rural-urban Mestizo dispossessed, the passage from Indian to Mestizo status must be addressed in some detail. I have not studied in depth the communal passage from Indian to Mestizo, or the interethnic relations in either mixed communities or in entirely Indian communities with neighboring Mestizo communities, but I can make some statements that may illuminate the matter. There are three main variables in explaining the passage.

First, the initial degree of acculturation (at the beginning of modernization) of the community has been a significant factor in the perpetuation of Indian communities: the greater the initial degree of traditionalism, the more successful the community in resisting modernization and secularization. At the onset of the Mexican Revolution, the great majority of the population of the tierra templada and the tierra fría was composed of Indian-traditional and Indian-transitional communities.

Second, the initial degree of regional marginality and isolation affects the transition of Indian communities. I do not mean simply distance and accessibility to urban areas, as in Redfield's (1930) original formulation of the concept of the folk society. Rather, regional marginality becomes an efficacious variable of ethnic passage only in conjunction with other factors.[15]

Third and most important, the availability of labor migrant work and accessibility to places of work affects the transition. The foregoing discussion makes abundantly clear the scope and overall significance of this variable (see also Nutini 1997).

Individual passage from Indian to Mestizo status, on the other hand, is a topic that I have studied quite extensively, and here I can make more definitive statements. First, the transition is most significantly determined by exogenous factors, primarily sustained contact with the outside world, in the context of labor migration or economic transactions. It should be noted, however, that the transition is also affected by endogenous factors such as primary education and television (during the past ten years, owning a television set has become fairly common in Indian-transitional and even Indian-traditional communities). Teenagers are the group that is most affected by these endogenous factors, and the most common manifestation of the ongoing process of Mestizoization is changes in dress (i.e., discarding altogether Indian garments and adopting the usual attire of urban youth, jeans and colorful shirts or blouses) and refusing to communicate in Nahuatl, which is encouraged by schoolteachers.

Second, individual transition to Mestizo status is much greater in Indian-transitional than in Indian-traditional communities, not only because the former is intrinsically more advanced in the process of modernization but also because labor migration is an established pattern and there is on the whole greater contact with the outside world. It is in the context of Indian-transitional communities that individual and collective factors coalesce and create the perception that the community is no longer Indian. Let me explain. There are two aspects of this juncture. On the one hand, in Indian-traditional communities modernization is weak, and the rebelliousness of the young is not strong enough to affect the community as a whole. The behavior of the young may affect the organization and functioning of the family, but it does not create the collective perception that the community is in a process of transition. This is because few teenagers rebel, and many of them leave the community permanently in search of economic and social opportunities, thereby without significantly affecting the collective structure of the community. On the other hand, in Indian-transitional communities, having largely gone beyond the constraints of tradition, every time individuals acquire and internalize traits from the outside world the cumulative affect of the process affects the community as a whole, but more significantly, it propels men and women to conceive of themselves as no longer Indian. The main motivation is the perception that being considered Indian detracts from the possibility of success in the wider world. Such is the effect of the racist devaluation of Indian culture that pervades much of Mexican provincial society.

Third, as a corollary of the second point, is the behavioral and psychological consequences of the transition from Indian to Mestizo status. The issue is complex. The first step in the transition may involve years of modernizing traits involving a large number of urban cultural inputs, but there comes a critical point when individuals make the conscious decision, not necessarily to deny their Indian roots, but to behave in a manner distinctly non-Indian. To put it differently, modernization ushers in secularization; that is, the modal personality of the individual begins to change.

The second step entails young people's influence on their families and others to follow their course of action: children are encouraged to learn the ways of the urban world, and kinsmen and friends are encouraged to engage in labor migration and whenever possible to acquire the goods and technology of the city. Exactly when this process becomes generalized in the community I have been unable to ascertain. Or, as I said above, I still do not know at what point in the process of transition the community may be said to have achieved Mestizo status.

The third and final step may be encapsulated by saying that individuals acquire a Mestizo persona. What does this final transformation mean structurally and psychologically? With respect to the former, there is a conscious effort of individuals to divest themselves of lingering Indian diagnostic traits, such as speech patterns, presentation of the self, standards of personal behavior, and, in general, any form of behavior and action that may indicate their recent Indian past (at this stage Nahuatl and traditional Indian dress are long gone). People are very ambivalent about denying their Indian past, which they rationalize as being inimical to their aspirations for a better life. At the same time, however, being fully aware of their Indian roots, they engage in various forms of expressive behavior to palliate the denial.

Durkheim's dictum that social facts must be explained on the basis of social facts alone has been the norm among most anthropologists. But there have been dissidents who have maintained that psychological facts play an important role in explaining social facts. This is most notably true in the domains of change and ethnic transformation. It is in this context that Pitarch's (n.d.) excellent elaboration of the Indian persona in Mesoamerica is extremely useful. In the transformation from Indian to Mestizo status, I follow several of his suggestions.

Fundamentally, the transition from one ethnic status to another involves the internalization of a new ontological perspective. This transformation is what I would like to call the acquisition of a new persona, which changes the worldview and pragmatic configuration of the individual and ultimately that of the community in the sustained process of change. In the following paragraphs I am concerned with the Indian antecedents of the Mestizo persona and its consequences.

The concept of persona entails that ontological complex of symbols (latent and manifest) and injunctions and constraints that individuals and the collective have epistemologically internalized. In other words, realization of the persona defines the cultural experience of individuals and social groups, the perceptions they have of the world around them, and the nature of the social order. Thus what is involved in the acquisition of a Mestizo persona is the discarding of the main tenets of the Indian persona and the creation of new ones. In the case under consideration, the concept of persona is the result of an antecedent (Indian) cultural configuration in a new economic and demographic context. That is, the concept of persona is rooted in a specific structural (Indian) context, which gives rise to a new ideational order (worldview), which in turn is the mainspring to creating a new (Mestizo) persona.[16]

Pitarch (n.d., 1) asserts, "Indian cultural difference resides in a particular conception of the person, in a characteristic ontology distinct from that of Westerners. With respect to ethnography, this implies that Indian theories about what is a true human being, and what is not, is a very important field for understanding Mesoamerican culture and social life" (my translation). The same obtains in sketching the Mestizo persona, with two main consequences. On the one hand, as individuals and communities distance themselves culturally from their Indian roots, they create a new ontological conception of humans and the social order that, by the time they define themselves as not Indians, and as the individuals and communities around them do so, a new persona has emerged. On the other hand, although the Mestizo persona retains several Indian aspects (particularly in its conception of the supernatural), by the time it is manifested in the city it has become essentially Western. In terms of class and ethnicity, the Mestizo persona ultimately crystallizes as the carrier of the national culture, and in this sense Mexico is a Mestizo culture, despite the functional survival of many Indian traits and modes of behavior.

Specifically, what does the Mestizo persona involve structurally and ideationally? The best way to answer the question is by indicating the ways in which it has diverged from the Indian persona. A few examples may be useful. First and foremost is the Indian magicoreligious view of the social and physical world: fundamentally, the world is experienced through the screen of supernatural forces that govern the world of existence. I am not implying that Indians reason differently from non-Indians, or that they have a non-Western logic, only that their logical reasoning is based on different assumptions, which naturally results in different outcomes. To the neophyte, this gives the impression that Indians are psychologically different—"prelogical," "nonlogical," and other expressions that are employed to convey how Indians reason differently from non-Indian ethnic groups, which in various degrees, so the folk wisdom asserts, adhere to a Western mode of thought. This epistemological (ideological) stand is the core of Indian identity, which underlies the people's behavior and action as a group and vis-à-vis all non-Indian groups. In this worldview, collective has primacy over individual behavior, and it is centered on the propitiation of a rather vast array of supernatural forces, which include both religious and magical personages, events, and practices.[17] This aspect configures all other aspects of the Indian persona and provides consistency to collective and individual behavior. This epistemological outlook has been engendered by the isolation and lack of economic opportunities that has characterized Indian communities since the formation of the Repúblicas de Indios (Indian Congregations) in the sixteenth century, which not even the 1910 Revolution was able to redress. Thus the following examples illustrate the ontological contexts in which the foregoing epistemological outlook is realized.

Since the establishment of Indian Congregations in the mid-sixteenth century, Indian communities have been isolated from the wider world. Much has been written about whether this was a wise policy, which was dictated by the Spanish crown mainly to facilitate the process of conversion and catechization and to ensure political control over the Indians. Since the establishment of the congregations, the Indians developed strong patterns of rejection of the outside world that remained constant until Independence, except during the second half of the seventeenth century when the Indians expected that the colonial system would become more receptive to their aspirations. It did not, and later on the establishment of the cast system increased their rejection of the world beyond their communities. With Independence, there was again a glimmer of hope, but by the mid-nineteenth century the Indians were sadly disappointed by the disastrous consequences of the Reforma Laws, when they lost much of their lands. The Indians' situation worsened during the Porfiriato, and the efforts of dedicated "cultural revolutionaries" after 1910 to incorporate the Indians into the national fabric of society were mostly unsuccessful.[18]

It has been in more recent times, after World War II, that individually and collectively Indians have increasingly made the transition to Mestizo status: some within originally Indian settlements, thereby becoming mixed communities; others by migrating outward or settling in nearby, already Mestizo communities. This transition has not been generated by actions of the government or nongovernmental organizations but by the process of modernization and secularization brought about by the construction of roads, transportation, communication, and other agents of change.

In this environment of isolation and rejection, the main component of the Indian persona was forged. Even today, the magicoreligious ideology of Indians continues to color their conception of the individual and its relationship with the outside world. Mistrust of institutions exogenous to the community, government intervention, and individual and collective self-reliance that interferes with traditional values, no matter how unreliable and far-fetched they might have proven in the past, characterize the organization of the Indian community. In other words, they rely on Catholic supernaturals in time of scarcity and stress rather than avail themselves of whatever help the government can provide (in most cases, not very much at the local level), on curers and sorcerers to stay healthy, and on communal cooperation and exchange to deal with immediate economic and material needs. In a nutshell, the fundamental institutions of the Indian community are magic and religion, kinship and compadrazgo.

The Indian conception of the human body is essentially of pre-Hispanic origin but is tempered by the effect of Western, Catholic beliefs and practices as embodied in the syncretic synthesis of pre-Hispanic polytheism and Catholic monotheism. This conception of the body has profound consequences for the organization of the community and its relationship to the external world. This aspect of the Indian persona needs to be elaborated in some detail.

My reading of Mesoamerican ethnography indicates that Indians make a transcendental distinction between the corporeal and noncorporeal constitution of humans, or, if you will, between body and soul. (I have elicited this conception among the least acculturated people in the Tlaxcala-Pueblan Valley and among Nahuatl-speaking Indians in the Sierra de Puebla and the Córdoba-Orizaba region.) Moreover, Indians believe that the soul of all humans —Mestizos, whites, and all non-Indians they come into contact with —have the same noncorporeal composition (the same soul), whereas what distinguishes an individual or a group from another is his or its corporeal attributes (individually, the body, the way it moves, what it desires; collectively, various cultural attributes such as diet and dress). How do these two interrelated beliefs affect the individual, the organization of the community, and its relationship to the outside world? Individually, they facilitate the adoption of non-Indian traits and practices, as long as they are reinterpreted and internalized according to the local cultural beliefs and practices. This aspect of the Indian persona has a positive integrative effect. This is particularly the case among the young, who are able to adopt all kinds of practices without unduly offending the majority of the community. The main sources of adoption are radio, television, and, to some extent, limited experience of city environments. Counteracting the individual integrative effects, the magicoreligious organization of the community still exerts a powerful pull toward traditionalism. When this delicate balance between individual acceptance and collective rejection is disrupted, the community is on the verge of transition to Mestizo status.

This may take years to materialize collectively to the point that the community may no longer be regarded as Indian, that is, when most people have acquired a Mestizo persona. To recapitulate, what does this mean? First and foremost, people cease to experience the world primarily through the screen of religion, magic, and kinship; they become secularized to the extent that other factors become progressively important in shaping their lives and in the decisions that must be made by new social and economic constraints. The end result is that they become culturally Mestizo, and the more propitious the social circumstances (physical mobility, direct contact with the city, and restructuring family life) and the greater the economic opportunities, the faster they become integrated into the fabric of the nation. The expressive analysis should specifically depict the change.

Interethnic Relations and the Indian Dispossessed

The Indians of the region, particularly those who live above an elevation of 1,200 meters, are the most dispossessed of the dispossessed. With little labor migration, the economy is based on subsistence agriculture, with a small amount of craft production. Less than 40 percent of this region is flat land, and most of the agriculture is practiced on mountain slopes, some of them having more than seventy-degree gradients, which must be cultivated by men secured with ropes. The material culture is simple. Houses are built of wooden planks, with tin-sheet roofs and packed-earth floors. Only in nucleated communities are some houses built of *manpostería* (mortar and stone). There are a few chairs and tables and occasionally a cupboard; there are some crude wooden beds, but the great majority of people sleep on the floor on *petates* (bulrush mats). Household utensils include a mixture of homemade earthenware pots and wooden articles and factory-made pots, pans, knives, and spoons. Most women have retained the traditional dress—which consists of an embroidered blouse and wraparound skirt, whereas men are giving up traditional dress—a white, loose-fitting shirt and pants tied at the waist and ankle—for factory-made shirts and pants.

Probably more than 30 percent of households are made up of joint and lineal extended families. Beyond the household, the only functional kinship unit is the nonresidential extended family (what Robichaux [1995] calls limited patrilineages), as few as four to as many as seven nuclear and lineal and joint extended family households living in close proximity. In dispersed communities they constitute the small clusters of households typical in the region of this type of settlement; in nucleated communities, they are located close to each other on the same block or along a single street. The nonresidential extended family has important social, religious, and economic functions, often of a corporate nature, in the life and ritual cycles. Kinship is the single most efficient principle-generating resource, and its most typical forms are institutionalized exchange, cooperation for religious and social events, and nonreciprocal labor exchange. Almost as important is compadrazgo, which complements kinship for the same purposes. The system varies somewhat from community to community, but it includes sacramental, primary nonsacramental, and secondary nonsacramental compadrazgo types (Nutini 1984, 3–16), and the average community has at least twenty types. (In fact, with the exception of the Tlaxcala-Pueblan Valley, the Córdoba-Orizaba region has the most diversified compadrazgo system in Mesoamerica, as exhibited in the ethnographic literature.) The complementarity of kinship and compadrazgo is a powerful force for maintaining religion as a traditional, well-integrated system. An example illustrates this assertion.

The rather distinct separation of the private and public aspects of the cult of the saints is a common trait of Mesoamerican Indian religion, the former centered in the household (or component households of the nonresidential extended family) and the latter in the community or municipal church. The more formal aspects of local religion (mayordomías, *hermandades,* or sisterhoods, the main events of the annual cycle and the rites and ceremonies that accompany them) always take place in church, and all members of the community may participate at will. The more informal, private aspects of religion (e.g., prayers, rosaries, burials, devotions) are discharged in front of the household altar, and usually only kinsmen participate. However, some aspects of the public cult (such as asking someone to become a *mayordomo* or a *fiscal* [main officials in the local religious hierarchy]) and several ritual events of the annual cult of the saints do take place in the household. In highly dispersed municipios such as Tequila this is particularly accentuated, whereas in nucleated communities such as Ixhuatlancillo there is a significant blending of these two sides of the dichotomy. Structurally more significant is that kinship is the main principle that generates the necessary resources for the private realization of religion, whereas compadrazgo networks are the main generator of resources and provide the organizing networks for its public realization. The highly dispersed settlement pattern of several municipios and the fact that kinship relationships are not effective beyond the nonresidential extended family is the reason for this division of labor, which, needless to say, is the rule in dispersed municipios.

Like other Nahuatl-speaking areas of central Mexico, the Indian population and residually Mestizo communities have an extensive magical complex, which I have elsewhere called anthropomorphic supernaturalism (Nutini and Roberts 1993). This complex includes elements and personages of witchcraft, sorcery, curing, and the worship of natural elements. It is almost entirely of pre-Hispanic origin and, more than in any other Nahuatl-speaking areas, contains elements of African witchcraft and sorcery. The most prominent of these beliefs and practices are several varieties of witches, most significantly a bloodsucking witch, known as *tlahuelpochi* or *tlahuapochin,* who, like its counterpart in the Tlaxcala-Pueblan Valley, specializes in sucking the blood of infants; several varieties of malevolent and benevolent sorcerers known respectively as *tuxtlachic* and *tetlachinec;* the omnipresent *nahual* (transforming trickster) known by the same term in most regions of Mesoamerica; and the worship of prominent mountains. Together with Catholic supernatural personages, this monistic supernatural complex is pluralistically discharged (e.g., the beliefs that govern the mayordomía system and the worship of mountains are the same, but the rites and ceremonies that accompany them are discharged separately). This exemplifies the essence of the Indian magicoreligious system.

The transition from Indian to Mestizo status is characterized by the disappearance or drastic diminution of the foregoing magicoreligious complex and attendant institutions and the acquisition, through variant periods of modernization, of a secular mentality that characterizes the Mestizo persona. In order of importance, the most salient institutions and traits that accompany this transformation are as follows. First, the magicoreligious system loses its efficacy; that is, individuals no longer experience much of the social and physical world through the prism of supernatural forces. Individuals retain beliefs and practices of witchcraft and sorcery but no longer in the context of a monistic belief complex. Second, the mayordomía system loses most of its public components and becomes centered in the household; individuals continue to celebrate the multiple feasts of the saints but mostly on an individual, nuclear, and extended family basis. The concept of public responsibility for sponsoring mayordomías, as a means of creating goodwill with the supernatural, disappears. Third, to a significant extent, compadrazgo replaces kinship as the main generator of resources for social and religious occasions. As a related aspect, once the belief associated with generating propitious conditions for existence with the supernatural fades, individuals begin to capitalize in economic terms. In summary, individuals and the collectivity become secularized (i.e., the supernatural hold on people becomes unimportant in securing personal well-being), and at this point the Mestizo persona, though retaining Indian elements, emerges as a distinct entity. For most working-class people, however, the process of ethnic transformation reaches its final stage in the context of the city, when individuals can be regarded as Mestizo and, however marginally, are part of the economic fabric of the nation.

To reiterate, the transition from Indian to Mestizo ethnic status is a continuous process that may take as many as four generations to accomplish. It is much shorter for individuals than for communities, and for the former it may take a single generation to achieve, which is attested by dozens of life histories that I have collected in an ongoing study of evangelism in the region. The main factor that accounts for the rapidity of individual transition is change of residence to an urban environment, particularly Córdoba. Perceptions of being an Indian are as important as actual material and nonmaterial changes in the transition. They are embedded mainly in language, dress, and certain forms of behavior that can be managed with relative facility and rapidity by Indians bent on achieving Mestizo status. Traditionally, men have been more adept in achieving Mestizo status, but women are catching up rapidly as increasing opportunities are available for women in the cities.[19]

Finally, what is the state of ethnic relations in the Córdoba region? Although the region may be characterized as an Indian-Mestizo dichotomy, it does not entail the rampant aspects of discrimination and exploitation characteristic in, say, the Sierra de Puebla (which I know personally) and in many regions reported in the ethnographic literature. There are clear-cut boundaries between Indians and Mestizos, to be sure, but there are no serious antagonisms and conflicts of interest in rural environments, as both occupy different agricultural niches that were established several generations ago. Moreover, most rural Mestizos, both the lower middle and working classes, are too close to their Indian past, and they know that their grandparents or great-grandparents were ethnically Indians, which diminishes discrimination and antagonism. It should be noted, however, that once individuals and groups perceive themselves and are perceived by others as Mestizos, they most emphatically assert that they have transcended Indian ethnic status. In the cities, the superordinate class and the solid middle class, having the working classes to exploit, perceived the Indians as a curiosity to show to visitors in their communities, doing nothing to improve their existence and lamenting the day when they will no longer have such forms of entertainment for visiting friends. To conclude, discrimination and exploitation of the Indians in the Córdoba region exists, but it takes place by omission rather than by commission.

Expressive Analysis

The Indian expressive array is focused mainly on magicoreligious reliance to achieve material well-being. This is the strongest centripetal force that keeps individuals and the community traditional. From this standpoint, the most important expressive domains revolve about propitiating Catholic and pagan supernaturals for favorable conditions for material existence: sufficient sustenance for family and kin, maintenance of an appropriate abode, and steady means to achieve these goals, without which there can be no harmonious social life, happiness, or contentment. This is the core of the Indian persona and worldview, created by the absence of internal economic opportunities and the perception that nothing can be expected from outside the community to ameliorate the appalling material and economic plight.[20] To put it differently, the mayordomía system, the cult of the saints, and the manifold propitiations of pagan supernaturals are the main structural domains for the realization of Indian expression. When this deeply ingrained, unconscious belief system begins to fail (i.e., when it does not produce minimally perceived results in alleviating the people's poverty), due to individuals realizing that opportunities are available outside the community, the process of modernization begins, and the locus of the expressive array, centered on magnifying and creating more opportunities, moves from the sacred to the secular domain. The ensuing analysis is concerned with secular, material, expression, relating primarily to Mestizoization.

Once the magicoreligious stronghold begins to wane, propitiation of the supernatural shifts to the material and focuses directly on specific items. Household items are most commonly the first to crystallize as means of expression: beds replace petates, store-bought articles replace traditional pots and pans, manufactured furniture replaces traditional items (benches, wooden consoles, hooks on the wall to hang clothes), and the house acquires a nontraditional look. The most diagnostic of these changes, as an indicator of transition, is the acquisition of beds, which almost invariably triggers the process. Household modernization is almost invariably accompanied by changes in language and dress: Nahuatl is still the main language, but Spanish is increasingly used in daily life; items of traditional dress are given up by men, and it does not take long for the complete transition to Mestizo attire (women take longer to undergo this transition). It is difficult to calculate the pace of modernization; it probably varies significantly, but in some cases the lapse between traditional Indian to transitional Mestizo may take a generation and a half or less.

I am not referring to entire communities but to limited segments of it. For example, two clusters of households (one with seven houses and the other with nine) in the dispersed municipio of Tequila were traditional Indian settlements in 1969; today, they are on the verge of achieving Mestizo status: their material culture is no longer Indian; all children are monolingual in Spanish, and most of the young people (between the ages of twenty and thirty) no longer speak Nahuatl fluently; all men and most women have given up traditional dress; and the clusters are well on the way of developing a Mestizo identity (and they are certainly regarded as different by neighboring clusters). I have not studied Tequila enough, but I intuit that Mestizoization proceeds by clusters and is uneven across the municipio. In nucleated communities and municipios, such as Ixhuatlancillo and Ixhuatlán del Café, on the other hand, the process of Mestizoization appears to be slower but more global (the entire settlement is transformed more or less evenly) and affected by other factors than in clusters of dispersed municipios. Be this as it may, the foregoing structural domains of Indian culture become the loci of realization of the expressive emulation that always accompany upward social mobility. These domains of expressive emulation are the most visible facts that mobility is taking place, and this particular case exemplifies how Mestizoization is proceeding.

Kinship in Indian culture is a vast domain of expressive realization, but in the process of Mestizoization compadrazgo assumes most of its functions as a generator of social and economic resource. Thus as compadrazgo becomes structurally more important than kinship, the former becomes also a more intensive domain of expressive realization. As an institution less constrained by prescriptive ties and physical location than kinship, compadrazgo, to function effectively, must be accompanied by a greater degree of expressive behavior. Searching for compadres, the preliminaries to contracting a compadrazgo relationship, the various rites and ceremonies that accompany the relationship, and the various patterns of interaction thereafter have an intense expressive component that is absent in the various institutionalized forms of kinship. As Mestizoization proceeds, and Indians, individually and collectively, give up and ultimately acquire a thorough Mestizo identity (most often in the context of the city), compadrazgo develops multiple subdomains of expression, the main form of which is expressive emulation. (This is a good example of why expressive realization is extremely important for the study of culture change.)

Labor migration is the main factor conditioning Mestizoization, which crystallizes with permanent migration to the city. The entire process is characterized by vicarious, expressive emulation, that is, patterns of behavior that configure the structural changes that take place as Indians become Mestizos and eventually urban working class. Indeed, in many cases, expressive emulation is the primary motivation for specific changes, namely, the desire to become like individuals and groups perceived in a superordinate position in the social and economic scale. Emulation is a powerful motivation that always takes expressive forms. Its most visible form is palliative, to assuage the unconscious denial of Indian ancestry: magnifying the individual sponsorship of mayordomías (i.e., making them more expensive and intentionally more ritually complex); exaggerating the ceremonialism of compadrazgo, as a surrogate of traditional kinship; and nostalgically, often unrealistically, remembering the Indian past. Thus palliative expression goes on until the Mestizo persona has fully emerged. But emulation has other more immediately observable forms, which are the direct result of acquiring expressive domains of Mestizo culture (such as learning manifold Mestizo kinds of behavior related to dress, language, and patterns of entertainment), not always successfully, as trying to adapt them to still latently strong Indian patterns of behavior elicits scorn from Indians and Mestizos alike.[21]

Nonetheless, after a core of these Mestizo domains has been internalized, like a domino effect, other material domains are incorporated into the changing context of emulation. Religion, kinship, and pagan supernatural beliefs and practices are the last to be affected by Mestizoization, and communities or fractions of communities undergoing this process may very often look more acculturated than they really are. In other words, assessing the degree of modernization and secularization as individuals and groups move along the process of Mestizoization requires a careful calibration of the interaction of material and ideational factors. In this operation, the expressive behavior this interaction entails is a necessary condition for understanding the transition from Indian to Mestizo status.

The transition to Mestizo status also involves the continuation of several social traits and institutions that by themselves are the source of expressive domains. This is the case, for example, with the nonresidential extended family, which greatly diminishes only when people settle permanently in the city. In the rural environment, a great deal of expressive behavior is centered in the nonresidential extended family, which has two main functions, to reaffirm this pattern of residence as an Indian institution (palliative expression) and as a transitional institution for rural migrant population (terminal expression). The same is true of marriage practices, kinship behavior beyond the family, and the celebration of the events of the life cycle.

The greatest structural changes in the Mexican stratification system take place in the transition from Indian to Mestizo status. This is shown diagnostically in the creation of a new persona that distinguishes these two ethnic categories, first in rural environments but acquiring definitive form in the city. Concomitantly, this combined process is manifested in modification and reorganization of the expressive array, the most visible aspects of sociocultural change. Hence the emphasis on expression in this study, for probably in no domain of culture is expressive behavior so closely related to change and transformation than in class structure and mobility.

Conclusion

*T*his book presents a description and analysis of social stratification and mobility in the Córdoba region. It is focused on the structural and expressive factors that have been instrumental in the class formation that has been taking place since the Revolution of 1910: the transformation from a highly stratified, nearly seigneurial system to a modern class structure, verging on that of contemporary industrial nations. A particular emphasis is the transition from Indian to Mestizo status and the crystallization of the latter in the urban environment.

ORIZABA IN THE REGIONAL CONTEXT
AND IN CONTRAST TO CÓRDOBA

Orizaba has a slightly larger population than Córdoba. It is located fifteen miles east of the latter and closer to the Citlaltepetl volcano. It is almost within the boundaries of what I have defined here as the Córdoba region and also has been a center for rural labor migration. Orizaba is conventionally regarded as having been founded in 1558,[1] sixty years before Córdoba, and dominated the region politically and economically until Córdoba came into its own as the regional market town at the turn of the nineteenth century. In the twentieth century there was intense rivalry between the two cities, as they developed different economies. The first factories, breweries, and foundries in the region were established in Orizaba, just before the turn of the twentieth century by English and French concerns and more recently by Mexican and American companies, most notably Kimberly Clark, which operates the largest paper factory in Mexico. Although Orizaba is a more industrialized city, Córdoba is more commercial (it caters to the agrarian needs of the region) and has developed as an important transportation center.

I did not include Orizaba in this regional study because, despite demographic and some wealth-generating similarities, the two cities are quite different in terms of stratification. This difference entails significant complicating factors in the study of the rural-urban dimension of class formation and mobility. Although my original research was formulated as the study of the Córdoba-Orizaba region and I gathered a considerable amount of data for the latter, I decided to write a separate monograph on Orizaba. Briefly, the differences between these two cities and their class structures is as follows.

First, the superordinate sectors are not the same. Although Orizaba has a few millionaires who made their money primarily in commercial enterprises, the factories are owned by corporations, and none of the major stockholders are enfranchised in the city. The wealth of the Orizaba plutocracy is not nearly as large as Córdoba's. Moreover, plutocrats from the Córdoba region regard those in Orizaba as poor cousins, somewhat uncouth and uneducated, and self-made men of humble origins.

The upper middle class arose after the Revolution and is regarded as socially inconsequential by Córdoba's superordinately placed. It lacks the social pedigree and tradition of Córdoba's and has none of the ties to the former landed aristocracy of the region. Orizaba's upper middle class does not have the expressive distinction and does not in any sense function as a group to be emulated as does Córdoba's. It is nothing more than an affluent group of merchants, businessmen, and a few professionals that in terms of wealth stands just below the lowest ranks of the plutocracy (i.e., their disposable incomes range from $200,000 to $400,000). (Indeed, Orizaba's upper middle class is essentially the structural equivalent to the upper middle class in the United States.)

The political class is structurally the same in both cities, with a few minor differences. For historical reasons, Córdoba has been politically more important than Orizaba. Beginning with the signing of the treaty of Independence in 1821 and about ten years after the end of the armed phase of the 1910 Revolution, Córdoba has been the political center of the region. There are more federal government offices in Córdoba than in Orizaba, but the state and municipal organization in both cities is identical.

Orizaba's solid middle class is smaller than Córdoba's, although the composition is the same. This is also the case with the middle and lower middle class, but Orizaba has a much larger proletarian class. The basic proletariat composition of Orizaba's class structure is explained by the earlier industrialization of the city and the large complex of factories it created. The most obvious characteristic trait of the city in this respect is the lack of cultural amenities, such as theater, music, and literary clubs, that Córdoba has to offer. Moreover, it does not have upscale sections where the plutocracy and upper middle class reside. In fact, many of Orizaba's elite families reside in Fortin, and much of their social life takes place with their counterparts in Córdoba. In general, the perception of Córdoba's superordinate and solid middle class is that Orizaba is an unsophisticated working-class city with none of the Culture (capital "C") they enjoy.

Irrespective of these expressive perceptions, during the twentieth century, Orizaba and Córdoba were equally important as centers of regional, village-centered, and permanent migration to the city. Rural folk have been migrating to these urban centers for more than a century, and it would be impossible to say which has played a more determinant role in the Mestizoization of the region. The earlier industrialization of Orizaba accounts for the type of labor migration that it attracted, which permanently marked it as a proletarian city; but this does not mean that it did not develop the range of classes described for Córdoba. The difference in the stratification systems of these two cities lies in the larger membership of the working and proletarian classes in Orizaba and the larger numbers of lower-middle-class and dispossessed persons in Córdoba. This difference is the result of different patterns of labor migration throughout the twentieth century.

While the class structure of Orizaba is more modern than Córdoba's (i.e., the alignment of classes is more consonant with that of medium-size cities in industrial countries), Córdoba has retained some aspects of the seigneurial, traditional stratification of the country. This is most noticeable in the configuration of the superordinate sector of society and the existence of a large and variegated dispossessed class. This polarization in the class structure is absent in Orizaba and may also be traced to the earlier industrialization of the city and the fact that in prerevolutionary times Córdoba was the regional hacendado city.[2]

THE SYNERGY OF INTERNAL AND EXTERNAL VARIABLES
IN CLASS FORMATION AND MOBILITY

In this section I focus on the confluence of variables that during the past three generations have been instrumental in the transformation of the regional stratification system, particularly on the passage from Indian to Mestizo status in rural and urban environments. The regional stratification system that has come into being is the result of government action and the opportunities that industrialization and commerce have generated, with the consequent growth of a very rich plutocratic class.

Beginning at the top, the sources of the industrial, commercial, and agricultural fortunes of the regional plutocracy are located in the demise of the hacienda system and the modernization of the region as part of the country's general process of modernization conditioned by the 1910 Revolution. This more open society created opportunities for the generation of wealth in the middle and upper sectors, massive social mobility in the lower rungs of society, and the necessary conditions for ethnic transformation, namely, the passage from Indian to Mestizo status, to a degree never before experienced in more than four hundred years of colonial and independent existence. The 1910 Revolution dealt a death blow to the seigneurial landed system and became a model and inspiration to subsequent revolutions in Latin American countries with large Indian populations.

The great wealth of local, regional plutocracies and affluent upper middle classes is the direct result of the fact that although the 1910 Revolution was a popular revolution, it was not a socialist one and developed opportunities for private enterprise. In other words, the states and the federal government created a new infrastructure that produced some socialist results, mainly primary and secondary education for the masses, greater access to higher education, and a system of health care and social security, whereas industry, commerce, most of the transportation and communication systems, and other wealth-generating sources were in the hands of the private sector. There are significant regional variations in these fundamental socialist-capitalist accommodations; in the Córdoba region, given its strategic location and its natural resources, it is not surprising that the local plutocracy is extremely wealthy. But are there other variables that account for this concentration of wealth? Essentially no, but many plutocrats today and the traditional upper middle class originally had a solid class position or were associated with the former hacienda owners, not to mention plutocrats of foreign extraction and politicians turned businessmen. At the top of the stratification system, idiosyncratic factors mostly account for socioeconomic mobility.

Educational opportunities account greatly for the formation of the solid middle and middle classes, as defined here. This sector of the regional class system, however, resulted from the industrial, commercial, and agricultural development of the region by providing the services and support that this complex economic system required. The doctors, lawyers, engineers, accountants, and many other professionals, as well as the owners of the diverse large and medium-size business concerns that are the property of these two classes, would not otherwise have come into being. This rather small (compared to the class structure of modern industrial nations) sector of the regional population is the key factor in gauging socioeconomic mobility. It is perceived by the great majority of the urban and rural lower middle and working classes as a realistic aim of upward mobility, and education is the main road to achieving it.

The lower middle and working classes have been the primary beneficiaries of the infrastructural services created by the state and federal governments. Free education, social security, and health services, albeit minimal, have been the main factors that during the past fifty years have transformed the majority of the region's subsistence peasants and urban dispossessed into active participants in the regional economy. As inadequate as the change has been and irrespective of the poverty that remains to be redressed, it is a far cry from the poverty and isolation that characterized the region two generations ago. Again, the relative prosperity of the region would not have been realized without the industrial-commercial transformation created by the private sector.

We can summarize the transformation of class structure and mobility in the region as follows. After 1919, when the armed phase of the Revolution ended, the government created a new infrastructure by providing education for the masses, building roads, and creating a safety net of health care and social security that provided the necessary conditions for the transformation.[3] The sufficient conditions for the stratification system's socioeconomic mobility were provided by the economic infrastructure created by the private sector. In my view, this was a good combination that would have been successful had it not been marred by chronic corruption at all levels of government and the private sector. What I have described for the Córdoba region, with minor differences, applies to countless regions of Mexico.

Finally, we need to explore how this confluence of variables affected the Indian dispossessed and how the process of change and mobility can be characterized. To some extent I have already answered this question, but I have not analyzed what is involved in terms of interrelationship of class and ethnicity. Despite the fact that since Independence in 1823 the law made no distinction based on ethnicity, as had been the case during the colonial period, and Indians de jure became citizens of the new republic, Indians remained a distinct ethnic group until well past the onset of the 1910 Revolution, despite half-hearted efforts to incorporate them into the fabric of the nation. The process of incorporation did not begin until the second half of the century, and although most Indian communities in the Córdoba region did not benefit from the ejido system, for the first time the increasing modernization and industrialization of the region presented Indian communities with potentially attractive economic conditions for the transition from Indian ethnic to Mestizo class status. These are communities that had not been dislocated by the 1857 Reforma Laws and the consequent growth of the hacienda system. To put it differently, from the French Intervention onward a process of limited ethnic change was at work that accounts for rural and urban Mestizoization and for the regional Indian-Mestizo dichotomy that has not yet entirely disappeared.

Implicit in the foregoing statement is that the transition from Indian to Mestizo status entails a fundamental change in ethnic perception. From the time individuals and groups are exogenously perceived as non-Indians and they endogenously have ceased to regard themselves as Indians (although they may be well aware of their origins and still be practicing some Indian customs), class becomes the main determinant of their position in regional society. Ethnicity does not altogether disappear and may have lingering effects in class formation and mobility. The point at which this transition becomes a fait accompli is difficult to determine empirically, mainly because phenotypically there are no perceptible differences between Indian and Mestizos, at least in rural communities, even when cultural Mestizoization has been occurring for three or four generations. This is a fundamental juncture to determine. After forty-five years of observing Mestizoization in several regions of central Mexico, I believe I have been able to conceptualize an adequate formulation of this process, but I am still unable to determine the specific synergy of factors and the point at which a community has made the transition to Mestizo status.

This critical point is easier to determine for individuals than for entire communities. Individuals, and occasionally entire families, who have acquired Mestizo status and are still enfranchised in Indian communities are easily identified for two reasons. They have acquired some diagnostic Mestizo traits, such as language or dress, that set them apart from the Indian majority, and the latter are quick to identify the former as having made the transition. The transition in urban environments always takes place in the context of permanent migration to the city, which almost invariably involves Indians already well along in the process of Mestizoization, so the transition takes place soon after individuals and

families arrive in the city. At least in the Córdoba region, I have not encountered Indians who have been enfranchised in cities for more than
five years.

It is quite another matter to determine when an Indian community
may be regarded as no longer Indian. The transition to Mestizo status is
usually gradual and may involve two or three stages that are difficult to
pinpoint. Also, there is the complicated factor of whether the region in
which the community is located has undergone sufficient modernization
that it can no longer be regarded as a region of refuge. More precisely, the
main factor to consider in the identification and transformation of ethnicity is whether the community is located in a region where an Indian-
Mestizo dichotomy (Aguirre Beltrán's [1970] *regiones de refugio*) obtains
or whether there is a distinct sociocultural continuum. In the former regions such as the Sierra de Puebla and the highlands of Chiapas, the
identification of Indian communities does not empirically present any
perceptual difficulties, and what Nutini and Isaac (1974, 377) call a
"static definition of Indianness"—that is, one based on a series of fixed
attributes such as speaking an Indian language, elements of material culture (dress, house types, etc.), and an element of self-identification—is
sufficient. In the latter regions such as the Tlaxcala-Pueblan Valley and
Morelos, the definition of Indianness is part of a dynamic process. What
does this entail? Essentially, the community must be placed in the context of the mechanism of modernization and secularization that makes
Indian communities change along the Indian-Mestizo continuum. Thus
Indian culture is conceptualized as an integral part of the culture and society of the entire region (i.e., it reacts constantly to external pressures
and is subject to corresponding internal reactions) and not as an isolated
entity, apparently in a state of inertia.

A third complicating factor is mixed Indian-Mestizo communities. In
most regions of Mexico there are not only mixed municipios but within
them mixed communities as well. In such situations, although living in
close proximity, Indians and Mestizos must basically be regarded as separate communities, for very often they have separate religious and social
organizations and quite often separate economies involving a good deal
of Mestizo control and exploitation of the Indians. Under such circumstances, the community is a microcosm of the region, and what I have
said about the latter applies to the former. One must be careful to assess
ethnicity, however, because the two groups ultimately share ethnic and
somatic origins that may go back many generations. In many cases the
origin of the local Mestizo nucleus is not local; it is composed mostly of

Mestizo families of nearby cities that settled in an Indian community, usually for economic reasons. These two origins of mixed communities affect differentially the process of class formation and mobility, due primarily to the more direct control and economic exploitation exercised by Mestizos. At least in the Córdoba region, the process of Mestizoization is faster in entirely Indian communities than in mixed communities.

To conclude, the configuration of rural society in the Córdoba region is not uniform. In the tierra templada and the tierra fría, the Indian-Mestizo dichotomy is still in place, and overall things have not changed significantly during the past two generations. This is primarily the result of isolation because of the lack of adequate roads and means of transportation until three decades ago, so that Indians have not been able to avail themselves of the new opportunities generated by the modernization and industrialization of the region. On the other hand, in the tierra caliente, a sociocultural continuum has been in place for more than fifty years, during which things have changed a great deal due to the significant integration of communities into the regional economy conditioned by an extensive and efficient system of roads and transportation. The result is that many Indian communities have become Mestizo communities, and it is difficult to discern what is Indian and what is Mestizo at the community level. In fact, the Córdoba region's tierra caliente has in most respects become quite similar to the Tlaxcala-Pueblan Valley.

RACE, CLASS, AND ETHNICITY

As Levine (1997, 13) rightly puts it,

> "Ethnicity" . . . is one of those concepts, like "culture," "custom," and "community," that social scientists use frequently but vaguely and idiosyncratically. Perhaps ironically, one of the earliest discussions of ethnicity, Weber's, provides a clear, concise treatment that focuses on the fundamental attributes of the phenomenon, and then rejects ethnicity as an analytically useful concept (Weber 1968, 385–398). Weber says that ethnic groups are "Those human groups which entertain a subjective belief in their common descent." He recognizes that people use a great variety of cultural traits, such as a language, religion, etiquette and morality, to articulate ethnic descent and often magnify these to define social boundaries. Since notions of common descent get manipulated so readily in the pursuit of political, economic or

other goals, and the ethnic dimension of social reality forms part of a wider social context, ethnicity "dissolves if we define our terms exactly" (1968, 395).

Weber's conception of ethnicity and Levine's apt characterization of it fit perfectly with the notion of ethnicity that I have assumed here. By itself, it is not a useful concept; to be an effective conceptual tool, it must be employed in conjunction with other variables. It can be manipulated to achieve individual and collective economic, political, even religious ends, particularly in the passage from Indian to Mestizo status. It must also be contextualized in terms of space and time — in the case of this book, in the rural and urban environments and in the various stages of modernization and secularization that the Córdoba region has undergone since the turn of the twentieth century.

My analytical standpoint here is that the Mestizo concept should be used processually, not as a bounded social or cultural entity; or, to put it differently, Mestizoization more appropriately denotes the dynamic nature of the concept. As I have emphasized, it is important to distinguish individual from collective Mestizoization, as individuals and groups move along a pluriethnic continuum from traditional Indian to secularized Mestizo. This standpoint also entails that the various categories of ethnicity are not fixed but part of this dynamic process, which is tantamount to saying that ethnicity disappears as individuals and groups acquire the subculture of usually superordinate groups, regardless of the ideological inputs that generated economic and, occasionally, political action.

This process characterizes the transition from ethnic to class categorization at the lowest level of the Mexican stratification system. This is only one of the uses or meanings of the concept, but ethnicity does not necessarily disappear when a class system is in place. As Indians in rural and urban environments become lower- or working-class Mestizos, race and national origins perpetuate ethnicity in the context of class formation and mobility. In the Córdoba region there are criollos, putative whites, and groups of Spanish, Italian, and Near Eastern origin with a significant degree of ethnic identity. But this is not the meaning of ethnicity that I outlined above, as one of the main thrusts of this book is to elucidate what happens to Indian ethnicity in the rural and urban environments in the context of class formation. I want to conclude with a few generalizations on the collective nature of this process, centering on the social, economic, and psychological (decision-making) factors that configure it.

Due to the synergy of the various exogenous factors affecting the community, as discussed in Chapter 5, and in an environment of relative isolation, collective ethnicity becomes largely a matter of exogenous and endogenous perception. This statement must be clarified. The necessary causes conditioning the passage from Indian to Mestizo status are structural variables (availability of better economic opportunities, accessibility to them, a more open social milieu, less control and domination from the outside; in short, a more open and propitious regional environment) that precipitate ethnic transformation. The sufficient conditions of the transformation, on the other hand, are expressive and ideological, that is, a new worldview (persona, if you will, as it was analyzed in Chapter 5) that is the consequence of the new regional, structural conditions that acquire independent efficacy on individual and collective choices at the community level. This analytical stand is posited on the assumption that the changing structural conditions of the region create a new ideology that makes it possible, for individuals and groups, to make nontraditional choices. This is the sociocultural environment in which ethnic identity changes, conditioning the transition from Indian to Mestizo status.

What traditional Indian communities internalize from the outside world are not really specific structural elements, patterns of behavior, or sociocultural traits such as clothing, new ways of planting and house building, or a new compadrazgo type but rather a new way of looking at things and organizing individual as well as communal life; and this new way has a primary economic component. This is what I call the new ideology (and the new persona it engenders), which not only modifies everything that falls under the rubric of economic behavior but all social behavior as well. People no longer structure their social perceptions in terms of the socioreligious screen of traditional ideology; and to the extent that the new ideology colors their social, religious, economic, and other types of behavior, we can say that it is gaining the upper hand and the traditional ideology is receding. This is yet another way to conceive the ambience in which Indians become Mestizos in the regional context.

What is the role of race in assessing social stratification, and how does this interact with class and ethnicity? The situation is as follows. At the extremes of the regional stratification system, phenotypic, somatic traits play an important role. Particularly at the top, phenotypic traits are determinant in class formation and mobility, and they lend themselves to the greatest degree of manipulation. There is a manifest belief that being perceived as phenotypically European greatly facilitates upward mobility

$\mathcal{N}$OTES

Introduction

1. This chapter is based on an outline of the Mexican stratification system presented in the conclusion to *The Mexican Aristocracy: An Expressive Ethnography (1900–2000)* (Nutini 2004).

2. On July 2, 2000, Vicente Fox, the candidate of PAN, was elected president of Mexico, ending seventy-one years of PRI political dominance. In forty-five years of fieldwork in Mexico, I have not experienced a more outstanding example of political awareness and involvement. There was jubilation in the streets, and people looked forward to a new era in which there would be good government and an end to corruption. Whether this will come to pass, it is difficult to say. My opinion is that there will be some beneficial changes: corruption will be curtailed at the top of the political system, and fortunes will probably no longer be made in politics. If nothing else, political consciousness has reached a point that will not permit the reelection of patently dishonest leaders at the top. However, at the individual, local, and provincial levels, corruption will not quickly abate, not until a considerable degree of citizenship has been achieved, and this may take another generation. Three days after the election, in the small city of Fortin, I randomly interviewed thirty working-class and affluent men and women about the election. A local barber put it best: "Es una ilusión pensar que con la elección de Fox todo cambiará. Los cambios vendrán cuando cambiemos nuestra manera de ser y nos volvamos más responsables" (It is an illusion to think that with Fox's election everything will change. Changes will come when we [Mexicans] change our ways and become more responsible).

3. This is not a particularly Mexican phenomenon; rather, it may be found in most Latin American nations, and in a more attenuated form it has survived in European countries. Even in Britain, probably the most tolerant and democratic country in the world, the traditional respect accorded to the aristocracy, and the awe that it still inspires, makes its stratification system perhaps the most rigid in Europe. Indeed, survivals of the estate organization of society are to be found in all countries in the Western tradition.

Chapter 1

1. In fact, aristocrats and Indians have retained several expressive traits that have essentially disappeared in the broad spectrum between these two extremes. Among them are a pronounced concern with keeping kinship ties neatly organized, a concern with genealogies, a strong ritual and ceremonial bent, and identification with the land as a symbol of identity. This makes eminent sense, for aristocrats and Indians are unquestionably the most traditional sectors of Mexican society and, except economically, the classes that have changed the least during the past three generations. Aristocrats and Indians know exactly who they are, and they have a high awareness of the sociopsychological aspects of class membership. All other sectors of the Mexican stratification system seem to be in a state of turmoil, as the system appears to be coalescing into a new realignment of classes.

2. It should be noted, however, that in the uppermost sectors of American society the situation is somewhat similar to the more rigid Mexican stratification system. But the upper middle classes in the United States are more exclusive in their behavioral interaction with those below them than the upper classes in Mexico are with all other classes in society. That is why place of residence, education, and civic affiliations are so much more important in determining class membership in U.S. society than in Mexican society, given the more ascribed nature of class membership in the latter.

3. I heard this folk saying for the first time in 1978 while investigating the Mexican aristocracy. One of my most perceptive informants told me the following anecdote: "Vivía en nuestras haciendas un indio muy ladino que decía que a medida que las gentes se acatrinan y hacen dinero se emblanquecen, y yo añadiría que los de su alrededor también los emblanquecen. Es por esto que a los pocos de nuestra clase que se les nota lo mestizo no se les discrimina y son iguales a los más güeros de nuestros aristócratas" (There lived in our hacienda a very sly Indian who used to say that as people acquire city ways and make money they become whitened, and I would add that those around them also whiten them. This is the reason why the few in our class who exhibit Mestizo physical traits are not discriminated and are the same as the blondest of aristocrats). Since then, I have heard variations of this saying many times in rural and urban contexts in central Mexico.

4. Notice that I have consistently used the term "European" and avoided the term "white." The reason for this is twofold. On the one hand, "white," as a racial category, is not used in Mexico with the same meaning as in the United States. The exceptions are contextual: occasionally to denote a culturally non-Indian individual at the local or regional level, or in the national urban and rural contexts to indicate fairness but not a somatic category. On the other hand, the term itself is loaded with social and cultural meaning, and this renders analysis more complicated. The term "white" in Mexico is essentially a cultural category that tends to bend as the occasion requires and seldom has a fixed denotation or core of denotative meaning.

5. The reverse of this situation has happened on a global scale in the history of the West. I have in mind the demise of the Roman Empire and the onset of feudalism two centuries later. Feudalism may be interpreted as the fragmentation of Western society into myriad folk societies in which the concept of citizenship that had been forged throughout the Roman Empire was lost. In the isolated, confining, and totally local ambience of feudal domains, the concept of citizenship ceased to exist and the worldview centered exclusively on the folk construct. As Western society evolved from feudalism to seigneurialism and on to the modern national state, the renewal of citizenship took place, but a strong sense of being a Frenchman, an Englishman, or a Spaniard took a long time to mature. In fact, the modern concept of citizenship reached maturity in most European countries only in the nineteenth century. It is therefore not surprising that it has taken Mexico (and most former colonies of European powers) so long to become modern, a situation in which you can properly speak of the great majority of the population as being citizens of the nation.

6. This situation, by the way, may be a universal aspect of colonialism and imperialism that goes beyond the confines of Western society and its extensions throughout the world. Witness the case of the Chinese.

Chapter 2

1. I vividly remember in 1958, when I began to work in Tlaxcala, visiting working-class neighborhoods in Mexico City. The phenotypical composition of the neighborhoods was no different from that of most Indian rural Tlaxcalan communities. It was not until years later that I realized why, when I learned that the genetic composition of the country was more than 80 percent Indian. Thus while Mexico may culturally be regarded as a Mestizo country, racially it is essentially an Indian country.

Chapter 3

1. There are in addition about fifteen individual millionaires with fortunes in the order of $10 million to $15 million. Some of them are descendants of traditional Porfirian families, but most are of rather humble origins who amassed significant wealth between 1960 and 1990, mostly in ranching, coffee production, and various large retailing concerns. I do not have much information on this group; their influence is not significant, they are not part of the regional ruling class as I have defined it here, and what I have to say about them will be discussed in the section on the upper middle class.

2. It is interesting to note that the ratio of individuals belonging to millionaire families to the total population involved is slightly higher in Córdoba than in Mexico City: 1,666 in the former and 1,883 in the latter. Whether this fact has any significance, I do not know, but I intuit the ratio may be constant for comparatively similar regions of Mexico.

3. This example merits an extensive endnote, for it exemplifies the colonial mentality underlying Mexican ethnicity that, despite the Revolution of 1910, has not entirely disappeared. In the 1880s the government of Porfirio Díaz engaged in a limited policy of European "colonization." In the words of the dictator himself, he wanted Europeans to come to Mexico "para mejorar la raza" (to improve the race) (Zilli 1980, 15–19). His idea was to establish a series of "colonias" (settlements) in various regions of Mexico, so that the residents would intermarry with local Mexican populations. The best known example is that of Italians imported in the early 1890s. Díaz apparently wanted immigrants from Latin countries in Europe but not from Spain, so he settled for northern Italians from the Veneto area, as he pointedly specified that he did not want southern Italians because, in his view, they were all mafiosi. Nearly two thousand immigrants arrived in Mexico and were settled in three communities: Mueva Italia, in the state of Michoacán; Chipilo, in the state of Puebla; and Manuel González, in the state of Veracruz. They were given land and the means to begin making a living, and by the early 1930s these were prosperous communities, as they are today (Alfredo Nanni, pers. com. June 1998). Two generations later, many had left their communities and become successful professionals; some had become millionaires, and a few occupied important positions in government and the private sector. However, Díaz's expectation was not realized, for neither in their communities nor in the wider world did they intermarry with Mexicans, and they remained highly endogenous. It was not until about thirty years ago that they began to marry Mexicans. In summer 1958 I surveyed the Nahuatl-speaking peoples in the states of Tlaxcala and Puebla, and I remember visiting Chipilo, an oasis of blond, Germanic-looking peasants in startling contrast to a sea of communities of typical Mexican Indian phenotypes.

4. This came to my attention in the course of researching the historical development of the Mexican aristocracy (Nutini 1995) and was later confirmed in investigating its contemporary expressive ethnography (Nutini 2004). One of the main social functions of the upper middle class since the rise of class stratification in the eighteenth century, and the gentry (its structural equivalent) before that, has been that of a support group, giving luster to the ritual and ceremonial life of the superordinate class. In my view, the explanation for this phenomenon is that the small membership of the aristocracy under the estate system, and that of the aristocracy-plutocracy under the global class system for the past two hundred, were and are too small to fulfill the social needs of exhibition and display that those who reach the apex of the stratification pyramid almost invariably develop.

5. Because this book is concerned with the social stratification of Córdoba and the region, it had to deal with the municipios that comprise the latter, since the postrevolutionary class system has been molded largely by migration from the countryside to the city. But I did not specifically investigate the political organization of what I have referred to as the local, folk context. And when I speak of the regional political class, I mean elected and past officials enfranchised in Córdoba and in five or six small cities and towns who have power and control over the

municipios of the regions but whose own political leaders are not part of it and have no input in regional decision making.

6. The distinction between being trained and being educated stems from the traditional conception of the university as a place of learning. The role of the university in Mexico is essentially to train students in all kinds of professions and fields of inquiry but not necessarily to provide them with what in the United States is called a liberal education, and consequently there is no distinction between college and university. From the first year in academe, the student concentrates on his or her professional or intellectual field of inquiry, and only incidentally is he or she allowed to take elective courses. The system basically assumes that education, in the liberal sense of the term, is the individual's responsibility, the rudiments of which have been acquired in high school or at home, and on which the individual may expand on graduation from the university. This worked reasonably well when a university education was the privilege of a few, but due to the policy of mass university education that the state has fostered during the past thirty years, higher education is becoming more and more like that of the liberal conception of education in the United States.

7. Elsewhere, I have extensively described and analyzed the somatic and phenotypic aspects of class and the relationship between class and ethnicity (Nutini 1997, 2004). Here I will highlight the main points directly related to provincial stratification.

8. Practically all plutocrats and upper-middle-class merchants of Near Eastern extraction are Christians and consider themselves of European origin. Whether this is true is difficult to say, but phenotypically they are unquestionably European. Exhibiting the same pedigree-enhancing syndrome observed among Mexico City plutocrats in the process of becoming aristocratized, two Córdoba plutocrats of Lebanese descent alleged they were descendants of thirteenth-century French crusaders. Far-fetched as this claim is, it is nonetheless similar to claims made by plutocrats and aristocrats in Mexico City in the context of expressive acculturation.

9. "Proper" and "elegant" are subjective terms whose meanings vary significantly across time and space. However, they, and a handful of other terms, are crucial concepts for understanding the role of expression in superordinate stratification (see Nutini 2004). They embody the essence of emulation, that je ne sais quoi desired by the majority of those who achieve structural (economic-social) status from the purveyors of superordinate expression to validate their new standing in society. To reiterate, aristocrats provided the basic expressive model for the national plutocracy in Mexico City, whereas the traditional upper middle class does the same for Córdoba plutocracy. This is the basic structural-expressive equation until the plutocracy begins to create its own expressive domains.

10. In at least a dozen cities in the country since colonial times (most notably Puebla, Guadalajara, Mérida, Guanajuato, and Oaxaca) there were large nuclei of aristocratic hacendados who thoroughly dominated the social and economic life

of the cities and regions in which their landed estates were located. The seven or eight hacendado families in the Córdoba region did not have the critical mass to constitute a local aristocracy, even though they had considerable social control of the city.

11. Since the eighteenth century, when the haute bourgeoisie emerged as a powerful industrial plutocracy rivaling the landed wealth of the aristocracy, plutocrats who achieved great wealth acquired many domains of the aristocratic expressive array as a validating mechanism of new social status. The expressive array of the aristocracy as the model to emulate remained undiminished until the second half of the twentieth century. In Western society in general since the middle of the century, and in Mexico in particular during the past twenty years, plutocracies have been creating their own expressive domains. A new expressive game is afoot, effectively terminating more than two millennia of the aristocracy as a model of expressive emulation.

Chapter 4

1. Permanent labor migration to the city beginning in the early 1920s has been the main factor in the tremendous growth of urbanization throughout the country, epitomized by Mexico City. All regional cities have been affected by the same phenomenon, and they are mini-replicas of the capital. The mechanics of the process in Córdoba are discussed below.

2. This situation became abundantly clear in questionnaires administered to more than six hundred respondents in Córdoba, Fortín, Coscomatepec, and four rural Mestizo communities. One of the questions was, "¿A qué clase social pertenece Ud.?" (To what social class do you belong?). My assistants and I kept asking the question, vainly hoping to get a sense of discrimination among the middle class, the lower middle class, and the working class. The answer, without the benefit of probing, was always the same: "Clase media."

3. The most numerous of these concerns are shoe stores, pharmacies, hardware stores, clothing stores, motels and hotels, restaurants, liquor stores, furniture stores, stationery stores, fabric stores, candy stores, toy stores, and sporting goods stores. Farmers, including ranchers (almost invariably urban residents), exploit spreads ranging from 100 to 300 hectares. Midlevel bank officials include managers of small branches, tellers, and other personnel above the rank of secretary. Bureaucrats include most positions above secretarial rank in the many municipal, state, and federal offices; professors teaching in the three local colleges; and principals of municipal, state, and federal primary, secondary, and high schools. In addition, SMC people in Córdoba own travel agencies, flower shops, art supply stores, gift shops, and other businesses commonly found in most medium-size cities in Mexico.

4. The economic affluence of the superordinate strata was computed in dollars and in terms of disposable income because of their great wealth. For the sake

of uniformity, I also compute the wealth of the middle stratum in dollars, but it is not meaningful to do so in terms of disposable income, except perhaps among the largest SMC businessmen whose incomes approach those of their upper-middle-class counterparts. Rather, it is more realistic to compute the wealth of the SMC in terms of gross income and approximate disposable income according to tax rates. Moreover, this procedure allows me to say something about the tax evasion that is common in all sectors of Mexican society.

5. This ranking is the result of an opportunity sample of twenty-five informants (equally divided among plutocrats and members of the upper middle class, the SMC, the lower class, and the working class) who were asked to rank the seven main professions. There was remarkable agreement among the respondents, but I do not entirely understand their logic, except in the case of lawyers ranking so low and the agronomists so high. Lawyers are perceived as basically dishonest and always prone to *tranzas* (shenanigans). It is probable that agronomists rank high comparatively because most people still idealize the land.

6. Admittedly, I may be wrong, but in the creation and fostering of citizenship and political democracy in modern nation-states, the SMC has played a crucial role. In the civil rights movement in the United States, for example, the SMC was instrumental in providing leadership and political support. Not so in Mexico since the 1910 Revolution. This phenomenon warrants close examination.

7. This practical rule also applies to establishing the earnings and wealth of the SMC and the superordinate sector. But because their economic involvement is to a significant extent in the public domain, it was possible to fairly reliably calculate the wealth and earning power of SMC businessmen and professionals and upper-middle-class entrepreneurs and plutocratic magnates. This is another way of saying that the economy of small lower-middle-class businessmen is largely underground.

8. The peso remained fairly stable during the period of data collection for this book (1993–2001). It ranged from 9.00 to 9.50 per dollar. Inflation, at least for Mexico, was low, never rising over 15 percent per year.

9. What this informant had in mind, as I elicited in subsequent interviews, was that Mexicans should respect the law, be conscious of other people's rights, not cheat on taxes, not pay bribes to facilitate business, and in general behave properly toward fellow countrymen. This is the conception of citizenship that, as I said above, will take time to develop and is independent of the party in power.

10. This attitude of lower-middle-class parents toward education was universal. Along the entire spectrum of the Mexican stratification system, with few exceptions, education is synonymous with training; that is, young people go to the university to secure professional (medicine, the law, engineering) or academic (sociology, history, anthropology) degrees, which will result in better economic opportunities and ultimately the means to rise on the social scale. The concept of a liberal education in Mexico is weak but not de facto that different from that of the United States, at least to judge from my experience of forty years of teaching

undergraduates. Be this as it may, this conception of education is basically the same in all social classes in Córdoba and the region. The superordinate class send their offspring to the university to secure degrees to run their businesses or make money on their own; the SMC, to secure professional degrees to maintain their socioeconomic status and to provide the means to facilitate mobility to the upper middle class; and the lower middle and working classes, to outgrow the social and economic status into which they were born. In this worldview, education is either nonexistent or has subsidiary importance. Liberal education notwithstanding, the same ideology, perhaps in different degrees, underlies the basic attitudes and concerns of Americans and Mexican parents and students alike.

11. This is one of the diagnostic traits in household decoration that indicates lower middle status. This elicits uppity derision of SMC people, cruelly highlighting the lack of education and cultural sophistication of lower-middle-class people. An analogous expressive faux pas obtains when SMC families cover their furniture with plastic, eliciting a similar reaction from upper-middle-class people. I could multiply twentyfold examples of expressive faux pas throughout the entire stratification spectrum that characterize the path of upward mobility everywhere.

Chapter 5

1. At the time of writing, the 2000 Censo General de la Nación (Mexican National Census) had not yet been published in its final form. Moreover, I was told from a reliable source that for Veracruz it was quite inaccurate. Thus all the demographic data used in this book are somewhat tentative and based on local (municipal) sources and information gathered from several federal agencies located in Córdoba.

2. This juncture is at the heart of explaining the communal passage from Indian to Mestizo status. It includes establishing at what point an Indian community may be said to have become Mestizo, what cultural baggage has been retained, and how it has been reinterpreted. As far as I am aware, there is no theory to explain this constant of Mexican culture, and I hope this chapter will contribute something to this thorny and ideology-laden problem.

3. Coffee production has diminished significantly during the past five years, and according to local agricultural experts, it will disappear as an important aspect of the regional economy. An agronomist at the local National Agricultural Station attributes this to a lack of field hands and the increase in wages, which makes the price of coffee produced in the region unable to compete with coffee produced in other parts of the world. This is basically the same phenomenon that is happening at the border with the United States: *maquiladoras* have been relocated in Asian countries where labor is even cheaper than in Mexico.

4. The more affluent of the rural lower middle class occasionally send their children away to high school and technical school in Córdoba, Orizaba, or more distant cities. Some of the most forward-looking families manage to send their

sons and daughters to college elsewhere in the state. All communities have primary schools for grades 1 to 6, and the largest ones have primary schools through grade 9, but there are no rural high schools. My research also suggests that rural primary and secondary schooling is not a significant variable in explaining upward mobility and change at the local level, and that is why I did not include education as one of the variables that has transformed the region during the twentieth century. It only becomes relevant when the rural dispossessed settle in the city, as the necessary background for furthering their education. All thirty-two rural dispossessed men and women (ages 20 to 32) whom we interviewed in the city and who were enrolled in educational extension programs had finished the ninth grade in rural schools.

5. This is not an obvious fact. In the Tlaxcala-Pueblan Valley the opposite is the case. With a proportionally even greater urban population than in the Córdoba region, the rural workforce of the Tlaxcala-Pueblan Valley is significantly larger than the urban workforce. The reason for this is that the Tlaxcala-Pueblan Valley has a longer and more extensive history of labor migration, and on the whole the valley is more broadly acculturated. A largely Indian rural population at the turn of the twentieth century has almost completely disappeared; only a handful of Indian communities remain today, and Nahuatl is still spoken by old people in less than fifteen communities. High population growth, poor quality of the land, and closeness to available places of work in the central highlands are the factors that explain this transformation, which are not present in the Córdoba region. In fact, the population of the Tlaxcala-Pueblan Valley may be described as a rural proletariat.

6. Throughout my forty-five years of anthropological fieldwork in Mexico, I have made it a requirement to interview children, mostly on the ideational aspects of culture. Their spontaneity has been a great source of information about which adults are reluctant to talk. In the present case, I interviewed about fifty children (ages 8 to 12), and more than half of them expressed resentment, some of them bordering on hate, of their parents because they favored or loved more ("querían más") the brothers and sisters who were physically different from them. They never specified what the difference was, but contextually it was evident that they looked more Caucasoid. This is a good example of the pain and misery caused by the endogenous racism that has been instilled in all sectors of society, which goes back to the Spanish Conquest.

7. I have encountered the same phenomenon in all the rural environments in central Mexico where I have done fieldwork. I have never entirely understood this behavior, but I think it has to do with keeping a low profile so that the rich do not elicit undue envy from fellow villagers. The syndrome of keeping up with the Joneses still takes place but never to the extent that is carried on in urban environments, where there is no community control to curtail it. Incidentally, this is a good index of rural secularization, that is, when collective social (and religious) controls no longer "unduly" affect the behavior of people and the passage to Mestizo-secularized status has been achieved communally.

8. The social and religious implications of folk religion and Christianization are analyzed in depth in a book on Todos Santos (Nutini 1988) and two books on compadrazgo (Nutini 1980; Nutini and Bell 1984) in the Tlaxcala-Pueblan Valley. With minor differences, they apply to the Córdoba-Orizaba region.

9. Class consciousness entails not only a sense of belonging to a social group and specific patterns of behavior but also collective action to safeguard or enhance the integrity and well-being of the class. In the Mexican stratification system, from top to bottom, the former are always present, but there is a notable lack of the latter. This aspect of stratification is related to a weak concept of citizenship, which, as I noted in Chapter 4, is only recently beginning to emerge.

10. This process of cultural homogenization has been the norm in modern industrial countries for nearly a century. In central Mexico, it has been going on since the late 1950s. In the Tlaxcala-Pueblan Valley, for example, the cultural distance between rural communities and the city in 1990 was practically nonexistent, at least in material culture, dressing, forms of entertainment, and a few other domains. This is happening at a fast pace in the Córdoba region.

11. Although my focus is stratification, it is necessary to touch on the expressive components of kinship as a significant aspect of class formation and social mobility. This is a constant in the Tlaxcala-Pueblan Valley, in the Sierra de Puebla, in parts of the Valley of Mexico, and in the Córdoba-Orizaba region. Moreover, the same obtains in the upper, middle, and lower classes in Mexico City, the city of Puebla, and several other cities in central Mexico where I have studied class structure and mobility. In fact, this is one of the most universal aspects of Mexican culture; the details vary from region to region and from class to class, but the general form remains the same.

12. Many societies have specific days or periods of time that may be characterized as "sacred," when activities depart from those of normal life. Examples of this institution are the Roman Lupercalia and the *treuga dei* (truce of god) in medieval Europe. In Mexican folk culture, sacred periods are common, and I have recorded them for rural Tlaxcala for Todos Santos (October 25 to November 9), for the Pueblan Valley (from Palm Sunday to the week after Easter), and for the Sierra de Puebla (from December 16 to January 6), and quite commonly for the day of the patron saint of the community. Another peculiarity of the sacralization of specific periods throughout the year is that they coincide with homecoming, which makes these periods extremely significant for understanding the changing nature of the community.

13. More than in any region in central Mexico with which I am acquainted is the city and the country so intimately socially and economically interconnected. In the Tlaxcala-Pueblan Valley, for example, there is more outward labor migration than in the Córdoba region, but city and country are rather clearly demarcated socially, economically, and demographically. Not so in the latter, giving the impression that rural communities are an extension of the city, as I have shown in this chapter. I cannot entirely explain this phenomenon, but I think it has to do

with the region being so small, connected by a good system of roads, with a local industry generating enough jobs, and yet relatively distant from major urban industrial centers such as Mexico City, Puebla, and the city of Veracruz. I intuit that this is a common pattern in many parts of Mexico.

14. My ethnographic experience in central Mexico indicates that the last aspect of culture to change in communities and regions is the ideational order. In Tlaxcala, for example, there are many communities that look outwardly secular (quite urbanized, with a modern material culture, and politically involved beyond the politics of kinship and religion), yet beneath the surface there is an active complex of witchcraft, sorcery, curing, and weather-making and a traditional (magic) religious ideology. I have observed the same phenomenon in the Córdoba region.

15. Since my ethnographic survey of the Tlaxcala-Pueblan Valley and the Sierra de Puebla in summer 1958, I realized that Redfield's formulation of the folk society, primarily in terms of distance to urban centers, did not work. In the Córdoba-Orizaba region, for example, Ixhuatlancillo is located eight miles from the outskirts of the city of Orizaba and remains today a traditional Indian community, whereas other communities, more isolated and located two or three times farther from Córdoba or Orizaba, have made the transition to Mestizo-secularized status during the past generation. To be an efficacious variable, distance from the city must be accompanied by other factors. The factors vary from region to region, but they have to do with the internal organization of the community, specific historical antecedents, and demography. These factors are highly variable and difficult to integrate into any analytical construct explaining transformation and change. Indeed, my inclination is that distance to urban centers should altogether be dispensed with in any analytical complex designed to explain change and transformation in Mesoamerica.

16. The foregoing discussion is based on the fundamental idea that in understanding any sociocultural transformation, what changes first is the ideational order (Nutini and Bell 1980, 371–378). What Indian communities in the Córdoba region have internalized from the outside world, launching them on the process of Mestizoization, are not necessarily specific structural elements—patterns of behavior, items of clothing, a new way of planting, technological implements— but rather a new way of looking at things and organizing individual as well as collective life; and this new way has a primarily economic component. This is what I have called the emerging persona [a new configuration of ideological elements and a new worldview], which modifies not only everything that falls under the rubric of economic behavior but all other societal behavior as well. People no longer structure their perceptions in terms of the socioreligious screen of Indian ideology. This is the transition from modernization to secularization that underlies the final step of acquiring individual and communal Mestizo status.

17. This is not the place to discuss the magicoreligious complex. Very briefly, it includes a main syncretic component of Catholic ritualism and ceremonialism

that has remained constant since the eighteenth century; a complex of witchcraft, sorcery, and curing of essentially pre-Hispanic origin; and elements of witchcraft and sorcery of African origin. This magicoreligious complex is essentially what Madsen (1957) has aptly termed Christo-Paganism.

18. Lest the reader misunderstand, since the onset of the congregations, individually and in large numbers, forced or voluntarily, Indians left their communities. An example of the former is the settlement of large numbers of Indians in the mining camps and cities beginning in the second half of the sixteenth century. An example of the latter is individuals and groups that settled in cities in search of better economic opportunities, such as Tlaxcalan Indians who by the beginning of the seventeenth century had established a distinct ward in the city of Puebla. Be this as it may, these processes of Indian outward migration, in various forms and with different intensities throughout colonial and Republican times, are the main factors that have redounded in the essentially Mestizo society that is Mexico today.

19. The transformation of communities and regions, particularly the transition from Indian to Mestizo status, has been an important concern for anthropologists working in Mesoamerica. The present book is in this tradition, and I would particularly like to acknowledge two predecessors, one rather early, Leslie (1960), and the other quite recently, Frye (1996). Leslie was one of the first. In his study of the Zapotec Indians of Mitla, Oaxaca, he described, among other things, the ideational aspects of the Indian transition to Mestizo status. Frye, on the other hand, in his study of Mexquitic in San Luis Potosí, addresses the nature of the town's identity in terms of the colonial racial ideology that still colors the perceptions of the people. Both of these are critical themes discussed in this book.

20. This well-justified perception is probably shared by most Indian communities in regions where the Indian-Mestizo dichotomy obtains, which the government policy of *indigenismo* after the 1910 Revolution has not been able to change. The transformation that Indian communities in many regions of Mexico have undergone has been caused by internal factors or the natural, serendipitous growth of industry and commerce in many areas of the country to which traditional Indian communities may have access by adequate roads and means of transportation. Not discounting education and radio and television, this has been the basic framework of modernization leading to the passage from Indian to Mestizo status.

21. In the process of upward mobility this is a common syndrome at all levels of the stratification system. The scorn that upper-middle-class people express verbally about some expressive behaviors of upwardly mobile solid-middle-class families is exactly homologous to rural Mestizos' derision of specific domains of Indians' expressive emulation in the process of becoming Mestizos.

Conclusion

1. Unlike the case of Córdoba, there is no specific date for the foundation of Orizaba. Spaniards began to congregate in the valley in 1535, and by 1569 it was

a regularly laid out town, which I have conventionally regarded as the beginning of the community. By 1580, with more than five hundred Spanish *pobladores* (original settlers), Orizaba became the district head town with a resident *corregidor* (crown official in charge of the political and economic administration of Indian congregations).

2. All these matters will be discussed in a forthcoming monograph on Orizaba.

3. Notice that I do not include land reform. Not because it was not necessary, but because of the form in which it was done. The *minifundio* (two or three hectares per family) that was the hallmark of the land reform, coupled with the absence of economic assistance that was the purpose of the foundation of the Banco Ejidal (which became instead a source of enrichment for politicians), perpetuated a system of subsistence agriculture that was neither good for the country nor profitable for individual *ejidatarios*. It took nearly seventy years to realize the inadequacy of the ejido system, and then it was de facto abolished. There were other ways to do justice to the landless peasants, which cannot be discussed here.

BIBLIOGRAPHY

Aguilar M., Alonso. 1983. *Estado, capitalismo y clase en el poder en México.* México, D.F.: Editorial Nuestro Tiempo.

Aguirre Beltrán, Gonzalo. 1940. *El señorio de Cuautochco.* México, D.F., Ediciones Fuente Cultural.

———. 1967. *Regiones de refugio: El desarrollo de la comunidad y el proceso dominuical en Mesoamerica.* México, D.F.: Instituto Indigenista Interamericano.

Aldana Martinez, Gerardo. 1994. *San Pablo Ixayoc: Un caso de proletarización incompleta.* México, D.F.: Universidad Iberoamericana.

Alonso, Jorge. 1976. *La dialéctica clase-élite en México.* México, D.F.: Casa Chata, Ediciones #3.

Andrade, Antonio R. 1966. *Córdoba 1966.* México, D.F.: Editorial del Heraldo de México.

Ariel de Vidas, Anath. 1994. "The Culture of Marginality: The Teenek Portrayal of Social Difference." *Ethnology* 41(3):209–224.

Aron, Raymond. 1966. "Social Class, Political Class, Ruling Class." In *Class, Status, and Power: Social Stratification in Comparative Perspective,* ed. Reinhardt Bendix and Seymour Martin Lipset. New York: Free Press.

Arriola Molina, Rafael. 1983. *Breve apuntes sobre la historia de la educación en Córdoba.* Veracruz: Revista Voces de Veracruz.

Baltzell, Digby E. 1966. "'Who's Who in America' and 'The Social Register': Elite Upper Class Indexes in Metropolitan America." In *Class, Status, and Power: Social Stratification in Comparative Perspective,* ed. Reinhard Bendix and Seymour Martin Lipset. New York: Free Press.

Bartra, Roger. 1974. *Estructura agraria y clases sociales.* México, D.F.: UNAM.

Bartra, Roger, ed. 1975. *Caciquismo y poder politico en el México rural.* México, D.F.: Siglo XXI.

Beals, Ralph L. 1954. "Stratificación social en la América Latina." *Ciencias Sociales* 5: 129–140.

Belmonte Guzmán, María de la Luz. 1987. *La organización territorial de Veracruz en el siglo XIX.* Jalapa: Editorial de la Universidad Veracruzana.

Bendix, Reinhardt, and Seymour Martin Lipset. 1966. *Class, Status, and Power: Social Stratification in Comparative Perspective*. New York: Free Press.

Boltvinik, Julio, and Enrique Hernández Lao. 1999. *Pobreza y distribución de ingreso en México*. México, D.F.: Siglo XXI.

Cabral Pérez, Ignacio. 1998. *Arquitectura del pasado en Orizaba y Córdoba, Ver*. México, D.F.: Edición del Autor.

Careaga, Gabriel. 1974. *Mitos y fantasias de la clase media en México*. México, D.F.: Editorial Joaquín Mortiz.

——. 1978. *Biografía de un jovoen de la clase media*. México, D.F.: Editorial Joaquín Mortiz.

Cardoso de Olivera, Roberto. 1992. *Etnicidad y estructura social*. México, D.F.: Imprenta de la Universidad Nacional Autónoma de México.

Carrión, Jorge, and Alonso Aguilar. 1972. *La burguesía, la oligarquía y el estado*. Mexico, D.F.: Editorial Nuestro Tiempo.

Colmenares M., Ismael, Miguel Angel Gallo T., Francisco González, and Luis Hernández, eds. 1985. *Cien años de lucha de clases en México, 1876–1976*. 2 vols. México, D.F.: Ediciones Quinto Sol.

Contreras S., Enrique. 1978. *Estratificación y mobilidad social en la ciudad de México*. México, D.F.: UNAM.

Cordero, Rolando, and Carlos Tello, eds. 1984. *La desigualdad en México*. México, D.F.: Siglo XXI.

De la Peña, Sergio. 1975. *La formación del capitalismo en México*. México, D.F.: Siglo XXI.

Florescano, Enrique, ed. 1985. *Origenes y desarrollo de la burguesía en América Latina 1700–1955*. México, D.F.: Editorial Nueva Imagen.

Friedlander, Judith. 1975. *Being Indian in Hueyapan: A Study of Forced Identity in Contemporary Mexico*. New York: Columbia University Press.

Frye, David. 1996. *Indians into Mexicans: History and Identity in a Mexican Town*. Austin: University of Texas Press.

Gillin, John P. 1945. *Moche: A Peruvian Coastal Community*. Institute of Social Anthropology, Publication 3. Washington, D.C.: Smithsonian Institution.

Gómez C., Francisco Javier. 1998. *Tánto que costó: Clase, cultura y nueva ley agraria en un ejido*. México, D.F.: INAH.

González C., Arturo. 1976. *Clases medias y mobilidad social en México*. México, D.F.: Editorial Extemporáneos.

González C., Gloria. 1972. *Subocupación y estructura de clases en México*. México, D.F.: UNAM.

Gutelman, Michel. 1974. *Capitalismo y reforma agraria en México*. México, D.F.: UNAM.

Harris, Marvin. 1964. *Patterns of Race in the Americas*. New York: Walker.

Henao, Luis Emilio. 1980. *Tehuacán: Campesinado e irigación*. México, D.F.: Edicol.

Herrera Moreno, Enrique. 1987. *El cantón de Córdoba*. México, D.F.: Editorial Citlaltépetl.

Instituto Nacional de Estadística, Geografía e Infomática (INEGI). 2003. *Mujeres y hombres en México 2003*. México, D.F.: INEGI.

Juárez Rivera, Hilda Margarita. 1987. *Capitales del estado de Veracruz*. Jalapa: Editorial de la Universidad Veracruzana.

Labastida, Julio, ed. 1986. *Grupos económicos y organizaciones empresariales en México*. México, D.F.: Alianza Editorial Mexicana.

Leal, Juan Felipe, and Margarita Menegus. 1995. *Hacendados y campesinos en la Revolución mexicana: El caso de Tlaxcala, 1910–1920*. México, D.F.: UNAM.

Leslie, Charles M. 1960. *Now We Are Civilized: A Study of the World View of the Zapotec Indians of Mitla, Oaxaca*. Detroit: Wayne State University Press.

Levine, Hal B. 1997. *Constructing Collective Identity: A Comparative Analysis of New Zealand Jews, Maori, and Urban Papua New Guineans*. New York: Peter Lang.

Lomnitz A., Larissa de. 1975. *Cómo sobreviven los marginados*. México, D.F.: Siglo XXI.

Lomnitz Adler, Larissa, and Marisol Pérez Lizaur. 1987. *Una familia de la èlite mexicana, 1820–1980: Parentesco, clase y cultura*. México, D.F.: Alianza Editorial.

López C., Francisco. 1967. *La estructura económica y social en la época de la Reforma*. México, D.F.: Siglo XXI.

Lopreato, John, and Joseph Hazelrigg. 1972. *Class, Conflict, and Mobility*. San Francisco: Chandler.

Luna de Carpinteyro, Fernando. 1991. "Bosuqejo de la población negra de Veracruz en el siglo XVI." Tesis de maestría, Universidad Veracruzana.

Lynd, Robert S., and Helen M. Lynd. 1937. *Middletown in Transition*. New York: Harcourt Brace.

Madsen, William. 1957. *Christo-Paganism: A Study of Mexican Religious Syncretism*. Middle American Research Institute Publication No. 19. New Orleans: Tulane University.

Martin, James. 1998. *Gramsci's Political Analysis: A Critical Introduction*. New York: Macmillan.

Martinez Asad, Carlos, and Sergio Sarmiento, eds. 1991. *Nos queda la esperanza: El Valle de Mezquital*. México, D.F.: CONACULTA.

Martínez M., Luz Ma, ed. 1995. *Presencia africana en México*. México, D.F.: CONACULTA.

Martínez N., Juan. 1984. *Conflictos estado-empresarios en los gobiernos de Cárdenas, López Mateos y Echeverría*. México, D.F.: Editorial Nueva Imagen.

Mendizabal, M. O. de. 1972. "El origen históricos de la clase media en México." In *Las clases sociales en México*, ed. M. O. de Mendizabal. México, D.F.: Editorial Nuestro Tiempo.

Muñoz, Humberto, Orlandina de Oliveira, and Claudio Stern, eds. 1977. *Migración y desigualdad social en la ciudad de México*. México, D.F.: Colegio de México and UNAM.

Nutini, Hugo G. 1968. *San Bernardino Contla: Marriage and Family Structure in a Tlaxcalan Municipio*. Pittsburgh: Pittsburgh University Press.

———. 1988. *Todos Santos in Rural Tlaxcala: A Syncretic, Expressive, and Symbolic Analysis of the Cult of the Dead*. Princeton: Princeton University Press.

———. 1995. *The Wages of Conquest: The Mexican Aristocracy in the Context of Western Aristocracies*. Ann Arbor: University of Michigan Press.

———. 1997. "Class and Ethnicity in Mexico: Somatic and Racial Considerations." *Ethnology* 36(3):227–238.

———. 2004. *The Mexican Aristocracy: An Expressive Ethnography, 1910–2000*. Austin: University of Texas Press.

Nutini, Hugo G., and Betty Bell. 1980. *The Structure and Historical Development of the Compadrazgo System in Rural Tlaxcala*. Princeton: Princeton University Press.

Nutini, Hugo G., and Barry L. Isaac. 1974. *Los pueblos de habla Nahuatl de la región de Tlaxcala y Puebla*. Serie de Antropología Social No. 27. México, D.F.: Instituto Nacional Indigenista.

Nutini, Hugo G., and John M. Roberts. 1993. *Bloodsucking Witchcraft: An Epistemological Study of Anthropomorphic Supernaturalism in Rural Tlaxcala*. Princeton: Princeton University Press.

Olivé Negrete, Julio César, and Beatriz Barba de Piña Chán. 1960. "Estudio de las clases sociales de la ciudad de México, con vista a characterizar la clase media." *Anales del I.N.A.H. 1957–58* 11: 153–195.

———. 1962. "Estudio de clases sociales en la ciudad de México: Experiencias con un grupo obrero." *Anales del I.N.A.H. 1961* 14: 219–281.

Othón de Mendizabal, Miguel, et al. 1975. *Las clases sociales en México*. 5th ed. Mexico, D.F.: Editorial Nuestro Tiempo.

Palerm, Angel. 1972. "Factores históricos de la clase media en México." In *Las clases sociales en México*, ed. M. O. de Mendizabal. México, D.F.: Editorial Nuestro Tiempo.

Paré, Luisa. 1977. *El proletariado agrícola en México: Campesinos sin tierra o proletarios agrícolas?* México, D.F.: Siglo XXI.

Pitarch, Pedro. n.d. "El lugar de la diferencia indígena: La percepción de la persona." Unpublished manuscript.

Pozas, Ricardo, and Isabel H. De Pozas. 1971. *El Indio en las clases sociales en México*. 6th ed. México, D.F.: Siglo XXI.

Ramírez R., Mario. 1990. *El sistema de haciendas en Tlaxcala*. México, D.F.: CONACULTA.

Rangel Contla, José Calixto. 1972. *La pequeña burguesía en la sociedad mexicana 1895 a 1960*. México, D.F.: UNAM.

Redfield, Robert. 1930. *Tepoztlán, a Mexican Village*. Chicago: University of Chicago Press.

Reyes E., Ramiro, Enrique Olivares, Emilio Leyva, and Ignacio Hernández. 1978. *La burguesía mexicana*. México, D.F.: UNAM.

Roberts, John M., and Brian Sutton-Smith. 1962. "Child Training and Game Involvement." *Ethnology* 1(2):66–85.

Robichaux, David L. 1996. "Le mode de perpétuation des groupes de parenté: La residance et l'héritage a Tlaxcala (mexique), suivis d'un modèle pur la Mesoamérique." Ph.D. dissertation, University of Paris.

Robson, Terry. 2000. *The State and Community Action*. London: Pluto Press.

Rodríguez y Valero, José Antonio. 1756. *Cartilla histórica de Córdoba*. Edición de Leonardo Pasquel. México, D.F.: Editorial Citlaltépetl.

Schama, Simon. 1989. *Citizen: A Chronicle of the French Revolution*. New York: Knopf.

Schwartz, Rami. 1994. *El ocaso de la clase media*. México, D.F.: Grupo Editorial Planeta.

Semo, Enrique. 1978. *Historia mexicana: Economía y lucha de clases*. México, D.F.: Serie Popular Era.

Sierra, Ma. Teresa, ed. 1999. *Dimensión Antropológica*, No. 15. Revista. México, D.F.: CONACULTA/INAH.

Sugiyama Lebra, Takie. 1993. *Above the Clouds: Status Culture of the Modern Japanese Nobility*. Berkeley: University of California Press.

Torres, B., Mariano. 1994. *La familia Maurer de Atlixco, Puebla, entre el Porfiriato y la Revolución*. México, D.F.: CONACULTA.

Tumin, M. M. 1962. *Caste in a Peasant Society*. Princeton: Princeton University Press.

Urías, Margarita. 1978. *Formación y desarrollo de la burguesía en México, siglo XIX*. México, D.F.: Siglo XXI.

Viqueira, Carmen, and José Urquiola. 1990. *Los obrajes en la Nueva España, 1530–1630*. México, D.F.: CONACULTA.

Wagley, Charles. 1965. "On the Concept of Race in the Americas." In *Contemporary Cultures and Societies in Latin America*, ed. Dwight B. Heath and Richard N. Adams. New York: Random House.

Warner, W. Lloyd. 1942. *The Saga of American Society*. London: Routledge and Kegan Paul.

———. 1960. *Social Class in America: A Manual of Procedures for Measurement of Social Stratification*. New York: Harper and Row.

———. 1963. *Yankee City*. New Haven: Yale University Press.

Whetten, Nathan L. 1972. "El surgimiento de una clase media en México." In *Las clases media de México*, ed M. O. de Mendizabal. México. D.F.: Editorial Nuestro Tiempo.

Wright, Edward. 1985. *Classes*. London: Verso.

Zilli, Juan. 1980. *Historia de la Colonia Manuel Gonzales*. Jalapa: Imprenta de la Universidad Veracruzana.

*I*NDEX